Arthur John Butler

Dante

His Time and his Works

Arthur John Butler

Dante
His Time and his Works

ISBN/EAN: 9783743320550

Manufactured in Europe, USA, Canada, Australia, Japa

Cover: Foto ©ninafisch / pixelio.de

Manufactured and distributed by brebook publishing software (www.brebook.com)

Arthur John Butler

Dante

HIS TIMES AND HIS WORK

By

Arthur John Butler

Late Fellow of Trinity College, Cambridge

Second Edition

London
A. D. Innes & Co.
Bedford Street
1897

PREFACE

THIS little book is mainly compounded of papers which appeared, part in the *Monthly Packet*, and part in the Magazine of the Home Reading Union. It will be seen, therefore, that it is not intended for those whom Italians call "Dantists," but for students at an early stage of their studies. To the former class there will be nothing in the book that is not already familiar—except where they happen to find mistakes, from which, in so extensive a field for blundering as Dante affords, I cannot hope to have kept it free. In the domain of history alone fresh facts are constantly rewarding the indefatigable research of German and Italian scholars—a research of which only the most highly specialised specialist can possibly keep abreast. Even since the following pages were for the most part in print, we have had Professor Villari's *Two Centuries of Florentine*

History, correcting in many particulars the chroniclers on whom the Dante student has been wont to rely. This book should most emphatically be added to those named in the appendix as essential to the study of our author.

In connection with some of the remarks in the opening chapter, Professor Butcher's Essay on *The Dawn of Romanticism in Greek Poetry* should be noticed. I do not think that the accomplished author's view is incompatible with mine; though I admit that I had not taken much account of the Greek writers whom we call "post-classical." But it is to be noted, as bearing on the question raised in the second footnote on p. 9, that most or all of the writers whom he cites were either Asiatics or nearly touched by Asiatic influences.

I have made some attempt to deal in a concise way with two subjects which have not, I think, hitherto been handled in English books on Dante, other than translations. One of these is the development of the Guelf and Ghibeline struggle from a rivalry between two German houses to a partisan warfare which rent Italy for generations. I am quite aware that I have merely touched the surface of the subject, which seems to me to contain in it the essence of all political philosophy, with special features such as could only exist in a country which, like Italy, had, after giving the law to the civilised world, been unable to consolidate itself into a nation like the other nations of Europe. I have, I find, even omitted to notice what seem to have been the ruling aims of at any rate the honest partisans on either side: unity, that of the Ghibelines; independence, that of the Guelfs. Nor have I drawn attention to a remarkable trait in Dante's own character, which, so far as I know, has never been discussed—I mean his apparent disregard of the "lower classes." Except for one or two similes drawn from the "villano" and his habits, and one or two contemptuous allusions to "Monna Berta e Ser Martino" and their like, it would seem as if for him the world consisted of what now would be called "the upper ten thousand." In an ordinary politician or partisan, or even in a mere man of letters this would not be strange; but when we reflect that Dante was a man who went deeply into social and religious questions, that he was born less than forty years after the death of St. Francis, and was at least closely enough associated with Franciscans for legend to make him a member of the order, and that most of the so-called heretical sects of the time—Paterines, Cathari, Poor Men—started really more from social than from religious discontent, it is certainly surprising that his interest in the "dim, common populations" should have been so slight.

The other object at which I have aimed is the introduction of English students to the theories which seem to have taken possession of the most eminent Continental Dante scholars, and of which some certainly seem to be quite as much opposed to common sense and knowledge of human nature as the conjectures of Troya and Balbo, for instance, were to sound historical criticism. Here, again, I have but touched on the more salient points; feeling sure that before long some of the scholarship in our Universities and elsewhere, which at present devotes itself to Greek and Latin, having reached the point of realizing that Greek and Latin texts may be worth studying though written outside of so-called classical periods, will presently extend the principle to the further point of applying to mediæval literature, which hitherto has been too much the sport of *dilettanti*, the methods that have till now been reserved for the two favoured (and rightly favoured) languages. Unless I am much mistaken, the finest Latin scholar will find that a close study of early Italian will teach him "a thing or two" that he did not know before in his own special subject; so that his labour will not be lost, even from that point of view. Then we shall get the authoritative edition of Dante, which I am insular enough to believe will never come from either Germany or Italy, or from any intervening country.

February, 1895.

CONTENTS

CHAPTER		PAGE
I.	The Thirteenth Century	1
II.	Guelfs and Ghibelines	16
III.	Dante's Early Days	38
IV.	Florentine Affairs till Dante's Exile	52
V.	Dante's Exile	69
VI.	The "Commedia"	89
VII.	The Minor Works	171
Appendix I.—Some Hints to Beginners		189
Appendix II.—Dante's Use of Classical Literature		198

DANTE: HIS TIMES AND HIS WORK

CHAPTER I.

THE THIRTEENTH CENTURY

THE person who sets to work to write about Dante at the present day has two great difficulties to reckon with: the quantity which has already been written on the subject, and the quantity which remains to be written. The first involves the reading of an enormous mass of literature in several languages, and very various in quality; but for the comfort of the young student, it may at once, and once for all, be stated that he can pretty safely ignore everything written between 1400 and 1800. The subject of commentaries, biographies, and other helps, or would-be helps, will be treated of later on. Here we need only say that the Renaissance practically stifled anything like an intelligent study of Dante for those four centuries; and it was not until a new critical spirit began to apply to it the methods which had hitherto been reserved for the Greek and Latin classics, that the study got any chance of development. How enormously it has developed during the present century needs not to be said. It may suffice to point out that the British Museum Catalogue shows editions of the *Commedia* at the rate of one for every year since 1800, and other works on Dante in probably five times that proportion.

Now, it has been said of the *Commedia*, and the remark is equally true of Dante's other works, that it is like the Bible in this respect: every man finds in it what he himself brings to it. The poet finds poetry, the philosopher philosophy; the scientific man science as it was known in 1300; the politician politics; heretics have even found heresy. Nor is this very surprising when we consider what were the author's surroundings. Naturally, no doubt, a man of study and contemplation, his lot was cast in the midst of a stirring, even a turbulent, society, where it was hardly possible for any individual to escape his share of the public burdens. Ablebodied men could not be spared when, as was usually the case, fighting was toward; all men of mental capacity were needed in council or in administration. And, after all, the area to be administered, the ground to be fought over, were so small, that the man of letters might do his duty by the community and yet have plenty of time to spare for his studies. He might handle his pike at Caprona or Campaldino one day, and be at home among his books the next. Then, again, the society was a cultivated and quick-witted one, with many interests. Arts and letters were in high esteem, and eminence in them as sure a road to fame as warlike prowess or political distinction. From all this it is clear that the Florentine of the thirteenth century had points of contact with life on every side; every gate of knowledge lay open to him, and he could explore, if he pleased, every one of its paths. They have now been carried further, and a lifetime is too short for one man to investigate thoroughly more than one or two; but in those days it was still possible for a man of keen intelligence, added to the almost incredible diligence, as it appears to us, of the Middle Ages, to make himself acquainted with all the best that had been done and said in the world.

This it is which forms at once the fascination and the difficulty of Dante's great work. Of course, if we content ourselves with reading it merely for its "beauties," for the æsthetic enjoyment of an image here and an allusion there, for the trenchant expression of some thought or feeling at the roots of human nature, there will be no need of any harder study than is involved in going through it with a translation. Indeed, it will hardly be worth while to go to the original at all. The pleasure, one might almost say the physical pleasure, derived from sonorous juxtaposition of words, such as we obtain from Milton or from Shelley, is scarcely to be genuinely felt in the case of a foreign language; and the beauties of matter, as distinguished from those of form, are faithfully enough rendered by Cary or Longfellow.

It may, however, be safely assumed that few intelligent students will rest content with this amount of study. They will find at every turn allusions calling for explanation, philosophical doctrines to be traced to their sources, judgements on contemporary persons and events to be verified. On every page they will meet with problems the solution of which has not yet been attempted, or attempted only in the most perfunctory way. For generation after generation readers have gone on accepting received interpretations which only tell them what their own wits could divine without any other assistance than the text itself gives. No commentator seems yet to have realised that, in order to understand Dante thoroughly, he must put himself on Dante's level so far as regards a knowledge of all the available literature. The more obvious quarries from which Dante obtained the materials for his mighty structure—the Bible, Virgil, Augustine, Aquinas, Aristotle—have no doubt been pretty thoroughly examined, and many obscurities which the comments of Landino and others only left more obscure have thus been cleared up; but a great deal remains to be done. Look where one may in the literature which was open to Dante, one finds evidence of his universal reading. We take up such a book as Otto of Freising's *Annals* (to which, with his *Acts of Frederick I.*, we shall have to refer again), and find the good bishop moralising thus on the mutability of human affairs, with especial reference to the break-up of the Empire in the middle of the ninth century:—

"Does not worldly honour seem to turn round and round after the fashion of one stricken with fever? For such place their hope of rest in a change of posture, and so, when they are in pain, throw themselves from side to side, turning over continually."*

It is hard not to suppose that Dante had this passage in his mind when he wrote that bitter apostrophe to his own city with which the sixth canto of the *Purgatory* ends:—

"E se ben ti ricorda, e vedi lume,
   Vedrai te somigliante a quella inferma,
   Che non può trovar posa in su le piume,
   Ma con dar volta suo dolore scherma."

It is hardly too much to say that one cannot turn over a couple of pages of any book which Dante may conceivably have read without coming on some passage which one feels certain he had read, or at the very least containing some information which one feels certain he possessed. A real "Dante's library"† would comprise pretty well every book

* Otho Fris., *Annales*, v. 36.

† A useful list, with some account of the authors cited by Dante, is given by Mr. J. S. Black, in a volume entitled *Dante;*

in Latin, Italian, French, or Provençal, "published," if we may use the term, up to the year 1300. Of course a good many Latin books were (may one say fortunately?) in temporary retirement at that time; but even of these, whether, as has been suggested, through volumes, now lost, of "Elegant Extracts," or by whatever other means, more was evidently known than is always realised.

We must, however, beware of treating Dante merely as a repertory of curious lore or museum of literary *bric-à-brac*—a danger almost as great as that of looking at him from a purely æsthetic point of view. He had no doubt read more widely than any man of his age, and he is one of the half-dozen greatest poets of all time. But his claim on our attention rests on even a wider basis than these two qualities would afford. He represents as it were the re-opening of the lips of the human race: "While I was musing, the fire kindled, and at last I spake with my tongue." The old classical literature had said its last word when Claudian

---

Illustrations and Notes, privately printed by Messrs. T. & A. Constable, at Edinburgh, 1890. He does not, however, include (save in one or two cases, and those rather doubtful) authors of whom Dante's knowledge rests on inference only.

died; and though men continued to compose, often with ability and intelligence, the histories and chronicles which practically formed the only non-theological writings of the so-called "Dark Ages," letters in the full sense of the term lay dormant for centuries. Not till the twelfth century was far advanced did any signs of a re-awakening appear. Then, to use a phrase of Dante's, the dead poetry arose, and a burst of song came almost simultaneously from all Western Europe. To this period belong the Minnesingers of Germany, the Troubadours of Provence, the unknown authors of the lovely romance—poetical in feeling, though cast chiefly in a prose form—*Aucassin et Nicolete*, and of several not less lovely English ballads and lyrics. Even the heavy rhymed chronicles begin to be replaced by romances in which the true poetic fire breaks out, such as the *Nibelungen Lied* (in its definitive form) and the *Chronicle of the Cid*.

In the new poetry two features strike us at once. The sentiment of love between man and woman, which with the ancients and even with early Christian writers scarcely ever rises beyond the level of a sensual passion,* becomes transfigured into a profound emotion touching the deepest roots of a man's nature, and acting as an incentive to noble conduct; and, closely connected with this, the influence of external nature upon the observer begins for the first time to be recognised and to form a subject for poetical treatment.† Horace has several charming descriptions of the sights and sounds of spring; but they suggest to him merely that life is short, or that he is thirsty, and in either case he cannot do better than have another drink in company with a friend. So with Homer and Virgil. External nature and its beauty are often touched off in two or three lines which, once read, are never forgotten; but it is always as ornament to a picture, not auxiliary to the expression of a

---

* I do not forget Ulysses and Penelope, Hector and Andromache, or Ovid's *Heroides*; but the love of husband and wife is another matter altogether. The only instance in classical literature that I can recall of what may be termed the modern view of the subject is that of Hæmon and Antigone. See, on this subject, and in connection with these paragraphs generally, Symonds, *Introduction to the Study of Dante*, ch. viii.

† This must be taken as referring only to European literature. Such a passage as Canticles ii. 10-14 shows that Oriental poets felt the sentiment from very early times. Is it possible that contact with the East evoked it in Europeans?

mood. You may search classical literature in vain for such passages as Walther von der Vogelweide's:—

"Dô der sumer komen was
Und die bluomen durch daz gras
Wünnecliche ensprungen,
Aldâ die vogele sungen,
Dâr kom ich gegangen
An einer anger langen,
Dâ ein lûter brunne entspranc;
Vor dem walde was sîn ganc,
Dâ diu nahtegale sanc;" *

or the unknown Frenchman's :—

"Ce fu el tans d'esté, el mois de mai, que li jor sont caut, lonc, et cler, et les nuits coies et series. Nicolete jut une nuit en son lit, et vit la lune cler par une fenestre, et si oi le lorseilnol center en garding, so li sovint d'Aucassin sen ami qu'ele tant aimoit;" †

---

* "When the summer was come, and the flowers sprang joyously up through the grass, right there the birds were singing; thither came I, on my way over a long meadow where a clear well gushed forth; its course was by the wood where the nightingale sang."

† "It was summer time, the month of May, when the days are warm, and long, and clear, and the nights still and serene. Nicolete lay one night on her bed, and saw the moon shine clear through a window, yea, and heard the nightingale sing in the garden, so she minded her of Aucassin, her lover, whom she loved so well" (Lang's translation).

or the equally unknown Englishman's:—

> Bytuene Mershe and Averil,
>   When spray biginneth to springe,
> The lutel foul hath hire wyl
>   On hyre lud to synge;
> Ich libbe in love-longinge
> For semlokest of alle thinge,
> He may me blisse bringe,
>   Icham in hire baundoun." *

But it is hardly necessary to multiply instances. By the middle of the thirteenth century the spring, and the nightingales, and the flowering meadows had become a commonplace of amatory and emotional poetry.

So far, however, poetry was exclusively lyrical. The average standard of versifying was higher, perhaps, than it has ever been before or since. Every man of education seems to have been able to turn a sonnet or ode. Men of religion, like St. Francis or Brother Jacopone of Todi; statesmen, like Frederick II. and his confidant, Peter de Vineis; professional or official persons, like Jacopo the notary of Lentino, or Guido dalle Colonne the

---

* Lud = song; semlokest = seemliest; he = she; in hire baundoun = at her command.

judge of Messina; fighting men, like several of the Troubadours; political intriguers, like Bertrand del Born—all have left verses which, for beauty of thought and melody of rhythm, have seldom been matched. But the great poem was yet to come, which was to give to the age a voice worthy of its brilliant performance. It is not only in literature that it displays renewed vitality. Turn where we will, in every department of human energy it must have been brilliant beyond any that the world has ever seen. It stood between two worlds, but we cannot say of them that they were

> "One dead,
> The other powerless to be born."

The old monarchy was dying, had indeed, as Dante regretfully perceived, died before he was born, and the trumpet-call of the *De Monarchia*, wherewith he sought to revive it, was addressed to a generation which had other ideals of government; but it had set in a blaze of splendour, and its last wielder, Frederick II., was, not unfitly, known as the Wonder of the World. The mediæval Papacy, though about to undergo a loss of prestige which it never retrieved, outlived its rival, and had seldom been a greater force in the political world than it was in the hands of the ambitious and capable Boniface VIII. The scholastic philosophy, which had directed the minds of men for many generations, was soon to make way for other forms of reasoning and other modes of thought; but its greatest exponent, St. Thomas Aquinas, was Dante's contemporary for nine years. These examples will serve to show that the old systems were capable to the very last of producing and influencing great men.

Meantime the new order was showing no lack of power to be born. Two of our countrymen, Roger Bacon and, somewhat later, William of Ockham, sowed, each in his own way, the seeds which were to bear fruit in the science and speculation of far distant ages. In the arts, architecture reached its highest pitch of splendour; and painting was at the outset of the course which was to culminate, more than two hundred years later, in Titian and Raffaelle. But in no field did the energy of the thirteenth century manifest itself as in that of politics. With the collapse of the Empire came the first birth of the "nationalities" of modern

Europe. The process indeed went on at very different rates. The representative constitution of England, the centralised government of France were by the end of the century fairly started on the lines which they have followed ever since. But England had never owned allegiance to the Emperor, while France had pretty well forgotten whence it had got the name which had replaced that of Gaul. In the countries where the Empire had till recently been an ever-present power, Germany and Italy, the work of consolidation went on far less rapidly; indeed, it has been reserved for our own age to see it completed. With Germany we have here nothing directly to do; but it is all-important to the right understanding of Dante's position that we should glance briefly at the political state of Italy and especially of Tuscany during the latter half of the thirteenth century. By good fortune we have very copious information on this matter. A contemporary and neighbour of Dante's, by name John Villani, happened to be at Rome during the great Jubilee of 1300. The sight of the imperial city and all its ancient glories set him meditating on its history, written, as he says (in a collocation of names which looks odd to us, but was usual enough then), "by Virgil, by Sallust and Lucan, by Titus Livius, Valerius, and Paulus Orosius," and moved him, as an unworthy disciple, to do for his native city what they had done for Rome. The result was the most genial and generally delightful work of history that has been written since Herodotus. Villani, who lived till 1348, when the plague carried him off, seems to have been a man of an equable disposition and sober judgement. Like Dante and all the Florentines of that day, he belonged to the Guelf party; and, unlike his great fellow-citizen, he adhered to it throughout, though by no means approving all the actions of its leaders. After the fashion of the time, he begins his chronicle with the Tower of Babel; touches on Dardanus, Priam, and the Trojan war; records the origin of the Tuscan cities; and so by easy stages comes down towards the age in which he lived. The earlier portions, of course, are more entertaining and suggestive than trustworthy in detail; but as he approaches a time for which he had access to living memory, and still more when he records the events of which he was himself a witness, he is our best authority.

CHAPTER II.

GUELFS AND GHIBELINES *

MENTION was made, in the last chapter, of the "Guelf" party, and this, with its opposite, the party of the "Ghibelines," fills the entire field of Italian politics during Dante's life, and indeed for long afterwards. It would be impossible in the space of these pages to follow up all the tangled threads which have attached themselves to those famous names; but since we may be, to use a picturesque phrase of Carlyle's, "thankful for any hook whatever on which to hang half-an-acre of thrums in fixed position," a few of the more prominent points in the early history of the great conflict shall be noted here.

* It seems proper to say that this chapter was written, and at least some of it printed, before Mr. Oscar Browning's interesting volume, *Guelphs and Ghibellines* (Methuen), appeared.

Guelfs and Ghibelines

As every one knows, the names originally came from Germany, and to that country we must turn for a short time to know their import.

About seven miles to the north-east of Stuttgart, in what is now the kingdom of Wurtemberg, is a small town called Waiblingen, where was once a stronghold, near the borders of Franconia and Suabia (or Alemannia), belonging to the Franconian dukes. Conrad, often called "the Salic," head of that house, was raised to the throne of Germany and the Empire in 1024. His line held the imperial crown for just a century, in the persons of himself and three Henries, who are known as the second, third, and fourth, or third, fourth, and fifth, according as we reckon their places among Roman Emperors or German Kings; Henry III. (or IV.) being famous as the great opponent of Pope Gregory VII.; Henry IV. (or V.) interesting to us as the first husband of the daughter of Henry I. of England, renowned in English history as the Empress Maud. The last Henry died childless in 1125. But the Franconian line was not extinct. Half a century or so before, Bishop Otto of Freising tells us "a certain count, by name Frederick, sprung from one of the noblest families of Suabia, had founded a colony in a stronghold called Staufen." Staufen, better known as Hohenstaufen, is a lofty hill about twenty miles from Waiblingen, and within the Suabian frontier. Frederick had been staunch to Henry IV. in his time of greatest difficulty, and received as his reward, together with the dukedom of Suabia, which the house of Zähringen had forfeited through disloyalty, the hand of the Emperor's daughter Agnes. By her he had two sons, Frederick, who succeeded to his own duchy of Suabia, and Conrad, who received from his uncle Henry V. that of Franconia, including no doubt the lordship of Waiblingen. At Henry's death Frederick and Conrad, being then thirty-five and thirty-three years old respectively, were the most powerful princes of the Empire. Henry had designated Frederick as his successor; but the electors thought otherwise. At the instance of the Archbishop of Mainz, between whom and the Hohenstaufen there was no love lost, and, as it would seem, not without pressure from Lewis VI. of France, whom Henry's death had just saved from having to face an alliance between England and Germany, they chose Lothar, Duke of Saxony.

We will now quote Otto of Freising once more. "Up to the present time," he says, writing of the year 1152, "two families have been famous in the Roman Empire, about the parts where Gaul and Germany meet, the Henries of Waiblingen, and the Welfs of Altdorf." The Welfs go back to by far the greater antiquity. They probably did not originally belong to the Bajovarian stock, for we read elsewhere that they had "large possessions in the parts where Alemannia meets the Pyrenæan Mountains," as Otto usually designates the Alps west of the Brenner. This Altdorf is a village near Ravensburg in Wurtemberg, between Ulm and Friedrichshafen. We first meet with the name in history about the year 820, when the Emperor Lewis I., "the Pious," married as his second wife Judith, "daughter of the most noble Count Welf." Somewhere about the middle of the tenth century, a Rudolf of the race was Count of Bozen. His son Welf took part in the insurrection of the Dukes of Worms and Suabia against their step-father Conrad II., "the Salic," and lost some of his territories in consequence, Bozen passing to Etiko, an illegitimate member of the same house. The family must have soon been restored to the imperial favour, for before 1050 Welf III. appears as Duke of Bavaria.

At his death, without issue, in 1055, he was succeeded by the son of his sister, who had married Azzo II. of Este. This Welf IV. fought on the side of Henry IV., against the revolted Saxons at the Unstrut, but soon rebelled himself. He became for a time the husband of the "great Countess" Matilda of Tuscany. Through him and his son Henry, "the Black," the line was maintained; and though during the period at which we have arrived the head of the family for several generations bore the name of Henry, it is usually spoken of as "the house of the Welfs,"* and the name is borne by some member of the family at most times. At the

* It may not be out of place here to correct the vulgar error that "Guelf" is in any sense the surname of our Royal family. The house of Brunswick is no doubt lineally descended from these Welfs of Bavaria; but it has been a reigning house since a period long antecedent to the existence (among Teutonic peoples) of family or surnames, and there is no reason for assigning to the Queen the Christian name of one of her ancestors more than another—"Guelf" more than "George."

accession of Lothar II. the head of the house was Henry, surnamed "the Proud." With him the new emperor at once made close alliance, giving him his daughter Gertrude in marriage. Henry's sister Judith was already married to Frederick of Suabia, but he sided with his father-in-law, and a struggle began which lasted for ten years, and in which the Hohenstaufen brothers had not entirely the worst of it. Conrad was actually anointed at Monza as King of Italy; but in the end, through the intervention of St. Bernard, peace was made, and lasted during the few remaining months of Lothar's life. At his death in 1137 Conrad was elected. His first act was to take the duchy of Bavaria from Henry, and bestow it on Leopold, the Marquis of Austria, his own half-brother, and whole brother to Bishop Otto, the historian. Henry died very soon, leaving a young son, afterwards known as Henry "the Lion," and a brother, Welf, who at once took up the quarrel on behalf of his nephew. He beat Leopold; but when, emboldened by this success, he proceeded to attack the Emperor, who was besieging the castle of Weinsberg, in Franconia, he suffered a severe defeat. At this battle we are told the cries of the contending sides were "Welf!" and "Waiblingen!" Why the name of an obscure fortress should have been used as a battle-cry for the mighty house of Hohenstaufen, we shall probably never know; it may be that it was a chance selection as the password for the day. However that may be, the battle-cries of Weinsberg were destined to resound far into future ages. Modified to suit non-Teutonic lips, they became famous throughout the civilised world as the designations of the two parties in a struggle which divided Italy for centuries, and of which the last vibrations only died down, if indeed they have died down, in our own day.

Of all faction-wars which history records, this is the most complicated, the most difficult to analyse into distinct issues. The Guelfs have been considered the Church or Papal party; and no doubt there is some truth in this view. Indeed, there seems to have been some hereditary tradition of the kind dating from a much earlier generation; long, in fact, before the Ghibeline name had been heard of. When, as we have seen, Countess Matilda of Tuscany, the champion of Gregory VII., was looking out for a second husband, she fixed upon Welf of

Bavaria, presumably the "dux Noricorum," who, as Bishop Otto tells us, "in the war with the Emperor, destroyed the cities of Freising and Augsburg." Their union did not last long, for Matilda seems to have been hard to please in the matter of husbands; but the fact of his selection looks as if he had been a *persona grata* with the Papal See. It is somewhat significant, too, that Machiavelli regards the contest between Henry IV. and the Papacy as having been "the seed of the Guelf and Ghibeline races, whereby when the inundation of foreigners ceased, Italy was torn with intestine wars." Yet we may shrewdly suspect that it was not so much any special devotion to the Church, as the thwarted ambition of a powerful house, which made the Welfs to be a thorn in the side first of the Franconian, then of the Suabian Emperors.* At any rate, when a representative of the family, in the person of Otto IV., at last reached "the dread summit of Cæsarean power," the very Pope, whose support had placed him on the throne, found himself

---

* Hallam considers that hostility to the Empire was the motive principle of the Guelf party in Lombardy; attachment to the Church in Tuscany.

within little more than a year under the familiar necessity of excommunicating the temporal head of Christendom. Still, in Italy no doubt the Guelfs, politically at any rate, held by the Church, while the Ghibelines had the reputation of being, as a party, at least tainted with what we should now call materialism. It will be remembered that among the sinners in this kind, who occupy the burning tombs within the walls of the city of Dis, Dante places both the Emperor Frederick II., the head of Ghibelinism, and Farinata degli Uberti, the vigorous leader of the party in Tuscany, while the only Guelf who appears there is one who probably was a very loose adherent to his own faction.

Less justified, it would seem, is the idea that the Guelfs were specially the patriotic party in Italy. No doubt the Popes at one time tried to pose as the defenders of Italian liberties against German tyrants, and some modern historians, forgetting the mediæval conception of the Empire, have been inclined to accept this view. But when it suited his purpose, the Pope was ready enough to support an "anti-Cæsar" who was no less a German, or even to call in a French invader. The truth is that at that time (and for many centuries afterwards), no conception of "Italy" as a nation had entered into men's minds. We do not always realise that until the year 1870, the territory, well enough defined by Nature, which forms the modern kingdom of Italy, had never, except indeed as part of a far wider Empire, owned the rule of a single sovereign. Patriotism hardly extended beyond the walls of a man's own city. Even Dante feels that residence in Lucca, Bologna, or Verona is an exile as complete as any, and that his only *patria* is Florence, though it may be safely said that to him, if to any living man, the idea of an Italian nation had presented itself.

The one argument which we can find to support this view lies in the fact that while the chief Guelf names are those of burgher families, many of the leading Ghibeline houses were undoubtedly of German origin. At Florence the Uberti, at Bologna the Lamberti, show their descent in their names. Villani tells us that the Emperor Otto I. delighted in Florence, "and when he returned to Germany certain of his barons remained there and became citizens." The two families just mentioned are specified. So far, then, the Guelfs may be regarded as representing native civic liberties against an alien feudal nobility, and the struggle between the two factions will fall into line with that which at a somewhat later date went on in Germany between the traders of the cities and the "robber-barons" of the country. In this aspect we may see the full meaning of Dante's continual allusion to the sin of avarice, under the image of the "wolf;" an allusion, again, which the original name whence the Guelf party took its appellation would specially point.

How and when the names first appeared in Italy we do not know. The first manifestation of resistance on the part of the cities to the Imperial control was given when Milan withstood Frederick Barbarossa—in defence, it may be noted, of its own right to oppress its weaker neighbours; but during the war which followed, and which was terminated by Frederick's defeat at Legnano, the head of the Welfs, Henry the Lion, was for most of the time fighting on the Imperial side, and though he deserted Frederick at the last, he does not seem to have given any active help to the Lombard

League. Yet it may well be that in his defection we have to see a stage in the transition from Welf to Guelf. It is, however, not in Lombardy, but in Tuscany, that the names of Guelf and Ghibeline, as recognised party designations, first appear. Machiavelli says—perhaps by a confusion with the Black and White factions, of whom we shall hear later—that they were first heard in Pistoia; but however this may be, they would seem to have been definitely accepted by 1215, to which year Villani assigns their introduction into Florence.

We have now reached the first date, it may be said, which students of Dante will have to remember; a date which to him, and equally to the sober chronicler Villani, marked the beginning of troubles for the city which both loved as a mother, though to the greater son she was "a mother of small love." The occasion is so important that it ought to be related in the historian's own words:—

"In the year of Christ 1215, one Messer Bondelmonte, of the Bondelmonti, a noble citizen of Florence, having promised to take to wife a damsel of the house of the Amidei, honourable and noble citizens; as this Messer Bondelmonte, who was a gay and handsome cavalier, was riding through the city, a lady of the Donati family called to him, speaking evil of the lady who had been promised to him, how that she was not fair nor fitting for him, and saying: 'I have kept my daughter here for you,' showed him the maiden; and she was very fair. And straightway falling enamoured of her, he gave her his troth, and espoused her to wife; for which cause the kinsfolk of the first promised lady gathered together, and being grieved for the shame that Messer Bondelmonte had wrought them, they took on them the accursed quarrel whereby the city of Florence was laid waste and broken up. For many houses of the nobles * bound themselves together by an oath to do a shame to the aforesaid Bondelmonte in vengeance for those injuries. And as they were in council among themselves in what fashion they should bring him down, Mosca of the Lamberti said the ill word: "A thing done hath an end," meaning that he should be slain.† And so it came to pass; for on the morning of Easter Day they assembled in the house of the Amidei by St. Stephen's, and the said Messer Bondelmonte, coming from beyond Arno, nobly clad in new white clothes, and riding on a white palfrey, when he reached the hither end of the Old Bridge, just by the pillar where was the image of Mars, was thrown from his horse by Schiatta of the Uberti,‡ and by Mosca Lamberti and Lambertuccio of the Amidei assailed and wounded, and his throat was cut and an end made of him by Oderigo Fifanti; and one of the counts from Gangalandi was with them. For the which thing's sake the city flew to arms and uproar, and this death of Messer

---

* Observe that the Bondelmonti were comparatively new-comers. They had originally belonged to Valdigreve, and had only lived in Florence for some eighty years at the date of this event. Hence they were looked upon as upstarts, and not properly speaking, nobles at all. See *Paradise*, xvi. 133-147.

† *Hell*, xxviii. 106. ‡ Possibly "by the Uberti lot."

Bondelmonte was the cause and beginning of the accursed Guelf and Ghibeline parties in Florence, albeit that before this the factions among the nobles of the city had been plenty, and there had been the parties I have said, by reason of the conflicts and questions between the Church and the Empire; but through the death of Messer Bondelmonte all the families of the nobles and other citizens of Florence took sides with them, and some held with the Bondelmonti, who took the Guelf side and were its leaders, and others with the Uberti, who were head of the Ghibelines. Whence followed much havoc and ruin to our city, and one may think that it will never have an end if God put not a term to it." *

The historian proceeds to enumerate the noble families who joined either side. Curiously enough, they were at first evenly divided—thirty-eight to thirty-eight. Not much is to be inferred from the names, though it is somewhat significant that of those, some half a dozen families in all, whom Villani, himself a Guelf, notes as having only recently attained to nobility, all joined the Guelf party. There seems also to have been a tendency for Ghibeline houses to become Guelf, which is not balanced by any defections in the opposite sense, so that the balance of parties was soon disturbed in favour of the Guelfs. At first, however, though

* Villani, *Croniche*, v. 37.

"there was a division among the nobles of the city in that one loved the lordship of the Church, and the other that of the Empire, yet in regard to the state and welfare of the commonwealth all were in concord."

This state of things did not last long. In 1220 Frederick II. was crowned Emperor at Rome. Up till that time he had been more or less a *protégé* of the Popes. First Innocent III., then Honorius III., had kept a fatherly eye upon his youth and early manhood, and for a time Church and Empire seemed to pull together. Honorius had, indeed, occasion to write severely to him more than once, but there was no breach of the peace. The accession of Gregory IX., in 1227, changed the aspect of affairs. Before the year was out, Frederick, like most of his predecessors for 200 years past, was under the ban of the Church: and from this time forward there was an end of peace and quiet government in Northern Italy. "Before Frederick met with opposition," Dante makes a Lombard gentleman of the last generation say, "valour and courtesy were wont to be found in the land which Adige and Po water; now may any man safely go that way, who through shame has left off to converse with good men or approach them." *

Florence seems to have remained longer than most of the chief cities aloof from the main contest. She had her own wars with Pisa, beginning with a private quarrel at the Emperor's coronation (in which we are expressly told that both parties united), and afterwards with Siena; and the great houses did a certain amount of private fighting; "but still the people and commonwealth of Florence continued in unity, to the welfare and honour and stability of the republic." In 1248, however, Frederick turned his attention in that direction, moved, it may be, by the growing strength of the Guelfs. His natural son, Frederick of Antioch, was sent with a force of German men-at-arms, and after some fierce street fighting, the Guelfs were driven out.

The Ghibeline supremacy was short-lived. Their nobles, especially the great house of the Uberti, became unpopular by reason of the exactions which they enforced; they got beaten in a fight with some of the banished Guelfs at no great distance from

* *Purgatory*, xvi. 115.

the city; and before the end of 1250 a meeting of "the good men," as Villani calls them, or, as we should say, the middle class, limited the power of the Podestà,* and appointed a Captain of the People to manage the internal affairs of the city, with a council of twelve Elders. Other important changes were made at the same time, and the new constitution—the third recorded in Florentine history—was known as the "Primo Popolo." The death of Frederick in the same year still further weakened the Ghibelines. Some of them were banished, and the exiled Guelfs were recalled. Peace, however, seems to have been kept between the parties for some time, and when in 1255 Count Guido Guerra on his own account expelled the Ghibelines from Arezzo, the Florentines restored them, and lent the Aretines money to pay a fine which the Guelf

* The name *Podestà* originally denoted the chief authority of a city or county, whether vested in one person or several. Frederick I. established Imperial officers under this title throughout Tuscany near the end of his reign, and for some time the Podestà was regarded as the Emperor's delegate. Before the end of the century, however, they had become municipal officers, gradually displacing the former consuls from the chief position. About 1200 the custom of choosing them from the citizens of some other town than that in which they officiated, seems to have become established; the native consuls being their councillors.

Guelfs and Ghibelines

chief had inflicted; "but I know not if they ever got it back," says Villani.

Again the compromise proved unstable. Manfred, Frederick's natural son, to whom, during the childhood of his young nephew, Conradin, the championship of the Hohenstaufen cause had fallen, was daily increasing in strength. His orders came to the Ghibelines of Florence to crush the popular party; and the latter, being warned in time, drove out all the great Ghibeline families. Two years later these had their revenge. On September 4, 1260, a date much to be remembered in the history of these times, the banished Ghibelines, aided by eight hundred of Manfred's German horse, seized the opportunity of hostilities between the Florentines and the Sienese to meet their opponents in a pitched battle. This took place on the Arbia, near the fortress of Montaperti, to the east of Siena.[*] The Guelfs were utterly routed, partly, it would seem, through the incompetence of some of the Elders who accompanied the army, and who, civilians though they were, overruled the judgement of the military leaders, and accepted battle under

[*] *Hell*, x. 96.

unfavourable conditions; and partly through the treachery of some Ghibelines who, not having been exiled, were serving in the Florentine host. Readers of the *Commedia* will remember the name of Bocca degli Abati, placed by Dante in the lowest pit of hell.*

Sixty-five of the leading Guelf families fled to Lucca, while the Ghibelines entered Florence, and appointed Guido Novello, of the great house of the Conti Guidi, Imperial Podestà. A meeting of the leaders of the party from Pisa, Siena, and Arezzo was held at Empoli, and a proposal was made on behalf of the rival cities, to raze Florence to the ground as a fortified city, and so preclude her revival as a Guelf stronghold. For once, however, a man was found to set patriotism above party. The great Farinata degli Uberti, whose wise counsel and warlike skill had mainly contributed to the victory, rose, with the same magnificent scorn, we may suppose, that Dante afterwards saw him display for the torments of Hell,† and let it be known that, so long as he had life in him, he would resist any such

---

* *Hell*, xxxii. 81, 106.
† *Ibid.*, x. 36.

measure at the sword's point. Count Giordano, the commander of the Germans, who had convened the meeting, gave in, and Florence was saved.

This was the last gleam of success which the Imperial cause was to enjoy in Tuscany for nearly half a century. Soon after the battle of Montaperti, Urban IV. was elected to the Papal See. He was a Frenchman by birth, "son of a shoemaker, but a valiant man and wise," says Villani. In view of the growing power of Manfred, vigorous steps had to be taken. The exiled Florentine Guelfs had made a fruitless attempt to effect a diversion in Germany, by inciting the young Conradin to oppose the acting head of his house. This old expedient having failed, Urban turned his eyes towards his own country. Charles of Anjou, brother of Saint Lewis, was at that time, next to the reigning sovereigns, the most powerful prince in Christendom, and to his aid the Pope appealed. Himself a man of Puritanical strictness in his life, and devoted to the Church, Charles was ready enough to accept the call, which appealed alike to his principles and to his ambition, and to act as the champion of the Holy See against the dissolute and freethinking Manfred;

and the influence of his wife, the only one of Raymond Berenger's four daughters who was not actually or in prospect a queen,* was thrown on the same side. After keeping Easter 1265 at Paris, Charles set out, and landed at the mouth of the Tiber in May. In December he was crowned at Rome King of Naples, Sicily, and Apulia. Two months later, at the end of February 1266, Charles and Manfred met near Benevento. After some hard fighting, of which the German troops seem to have borne the brunt, the battle was decided against Manfred by the desertion of his Apulian barons, and he himself was slain. His defeat gave the final blow to the Ghibeline cause in Tuscany. Only Pisa and Siena remained faithful. In Florence an attempt was made to avoid civil strife by the device of doubling the office of Podestà. Two gentlemen from Bologna, Catalano de' Malavolti and Loderingo de' Landolò, a Guelf and a Ghibeline,† were appointed, and they

---

* *Paradise*, vi. 133.

† They seem to have acted on the principle of filling their own pockets, rather than of maintaining order; and are placed by Dante among the hypocrites, in the sixth pit of Malebolge (*Hell*, xxiii. 103). They belonged to the order of Knights of St. Mary, popularly called Jovial Friars.

nominated a council of thirty-six, chosen from both sides. But this plan did not work well. Party spirit had grown too violent to allow of half measures, and before the year was out the people rose again, and the Ghibelines were banished for good and all.

CHAPTER III.

DANTE'S EARLY DAYS

IN the month when Charles of Anjou sailed up the Tiber to Rome, a child was born at Florence to a citizen named Alighiero, son of Bellincione. We do not know for certain his *casato*, or family name. Bellincione's father was another Alighiero, or, as it was originally written, Aldighiero. His father was Cacciaguida, who had a brother named Eliseo; from which it has been conjectured that he may have belonged to the prominent house of the Elisei, which is known to have existed as far back as the beginning of the eleventh century, since it was not uncommon for members of a family to bear the founder's name. We know, further, that the name of Alighiero came into the family with Cacciaguida's wife, who belonged to some city near the Po, probably Ferrara, where a family of Aldighieri is known to have existed.* In any case, it was originally no Florentine name, and it may be doubted if it ever was recognised as the appellation of a family. True, Dante is once or twice referred to as "Dantes de Alegheriis," but this may be due to the fact that he was known to have had recently two ancestors of the name. He himself, if we may trust the evidence of letters ascribed to him, seems to have written "Dantes Alligherius," while his son calls him Dantes Aligherii, and himself Petrus Dantis Aligherii, "Peter, son of Dante, son of Alighiero." In the official Florentine documents, where his name occurs, it is "Dantes Allegherii" or "Dante d'Alighiero," "Dante the son of Alighiero," and no more. The form "degli Alighieri," which would indicate a true family name, we find in no undoubtedly contemporary document.

In view of this initial uncertainty, the discussion whether the poet was of "noble" family or not seems a trifle superfluous. His great-great-grand-

* It may be noted that the name is undoubtedly Teutonic. The suggested derivations from *aliger*, "the wing-bearer," and the like, are purely fanciful. The first part of the word is doubtless *all*, "old," which we have in our own Aldhelm; the termination is the *geirr*, or *gar*, which occurs in all Teutonic languages, and means "spear." Dante (= Durante) was a common Christian name.

father, Cacciaguida, is made to say (*Par.*, xv. 140) that he himself received knighthood from the Emperor Conrad III. (of Hohenstaufen). This would confer nobility; but it would appear that it would be possible for later generations to lose that status, and there are some indications that Dante was sensitive on this point. At any rate, it is pretty clear that his immediate ancestors were not in any way distinguished. The very fact that he was born in Florence during a period when all the leading Guelfs were in exile shows that Alighiero was not considered by the dominant Ghibelines a person of too great importance to be allowed to remain undisturbed in the city.

Of Dante's boyhood and early youth we have only stray indications, and those mainly gathered from his own writings. We can, indeed, form a pretty clear notion of what he *was*, but we know little enough about what he *did*. From a very early period he was made a hero of romance. Without going so far as some recent writers, both German and Italian, who seem to look upon every statement of early biographers with suspicion, while regarding their silence as good evidence that what they do not mention cannot have happened, we must admit that we cannot with certainty date any event in the first thirty years of Dante's life. Still, we can infer a good deal. He must unquestionably, during this time, have read a great deal, for it would have been impossible for a man wandering about from place to place, and intermittently busied in political affairs, to have amassed in seven or eight years the amount of learning which the *Commedia* by itself shows him to have possessed. He must have been recognised at an early age as a young man of marked ability. His intimacy with the old statesman Brunetto Latini, who died in 1294, and his friendship with Charles of Anjou's grandson, Carlo Martello,* the young King of Hungary, who was at Florence in the same year and the following, are sufficient to prove this. Neither Brunetto, the most learned man of his age in Florence, and, as we should say, a man of "society" as well, nor a prince who, had he lived, would have been one of the most important

* Doubts have even been thrown on Dante's friendship with this young King. To these we can only reply that, if it is not implied by *Par.*, viii. 55, it is impossible to draw any inference whatever as to Dante's life from any line of the poem.

personages in Europe, was likely to have distinguished with his friendship a young man of twenty-nine, not of the highest birth, unless he had already made himself notable for intellectual eminence.

One event occurred during Dante's youth, in which he is so generally believed to have borne a part, that it will probably come as a shock to many people to learn that this belief rests only on the statement of a writer who was not born till nearly fifty years after Dante's death. On St. Barnabas's day, June 11, 1289, the Florentine Guelfs met the Ghibelines of Arezzo, in whose ranks many of their own exiles were fighting, in a plain called Campaldino, belonging to the district of Certomondo, which lies in the Casentino, or upper part of the Arno valley. The Florentines gained a complete victory, though only after a hard fight, in which many of the chief Ghibeline leaders lost their lives. The event was one of great importance, and Villani recounts it in very full detail.* Dante

---

* The conclusion of his account is picturesque enough to deserve reproduction. "The news of the said victory came to Florence the very day and hour when it took place; for the Lords Priors having after dinner gone to sleep and rest, by reason of the anxiety and watching of the past night, suddenly came a knock

also refers to it in one of the best-known passages of the *Purgatory* (v. 92). It is quite possible that he himself may have taken part in the battle; but if he did so, it is somewhat strange that none of the earlier commentators, including his own son, nor any biographer of the fourteenth century, should have known of it, or, knowing of it, should have thought it worth recording; and that it should have been left to Leonardo Bruni of Arezzo, writing after the year 1400, to make the first reference to so noteworthy an incident in Dante's early career. Leonardo (whose "Life" will be found in Bianchi's edition of the *Commedia*) quotes, indeed, a letter, said to have been written many years afterwards by Dante, in which reference is made to his presence in the battle; but this letter has long disappeared, and it is to be noted that the biographer does not even profess to have seen it himself. There is, it must be said, in the *Hell* (xxii. *init.*) one allusion

---

at the door of the chamber, with a cry, 'Rise up, for the Aretines are discomfited;' and when they were risen, and the door opened, they found no man, and their servants without had heard nothing. Whence it was held a great and notable marvel, seeing that before any person came from the host with the news, it was towards the hour of vespers."

to warlike operations in the Aretine territory of which Dante claims to have been an eye-witness; but as none of the early commentators seems to refer to Campaldino in connection with this passage, it tells, if anything, against the received story.

Another event, sometimes assigned to the period of Dante's life before his banishment, has somewhat more evidence in its favour. That he visited Paris at least once in the course of his life, the early authorities are agreed; but Villani, Boccaccio, and Benvenuto of Imola, all writing in the fourteenth century, make the visit to have taken place during his exile. It is not until we come to John of Serravalle, Lord of Fermo, who as Bishop of Rimini attended the Council of Constance, and there, at the request of the Bishops of Bath and Wells and Salisbury, prepared a Latin version of the *Commedia* with commentary, that we find mention of an earlier visit. His testimony is a little suspicious, because in the same sentence he also asserts that Dante studied at Oxford, a statement which, without strong confirmation, it would be very hard to accept. On the other side, it may be said that the silence of the older biographers is not conclusive evidence against the early study at Paris. Dante also went to Bologna, as it would appear, both before and after his banishment; yet while Villani and Boccaccio only name the latter visit, Benvenuto speaks only of the former. It is therefore quite possible that all three may have ignored the first period of study at Paris, or, if there was but one such period, may have assigned it to the wrong part of Dante's life. *Primâ facie* it is more probable that he would have undertaken both the long journey and the course of study in his days of "greater freedom and less responsibility," than when he was not only engaged upon the composition both of his great poem and of several prose treatises, but was taking an active share in political work.

Again, the allusion in the *Paradise* to the lectures of Sigier bears all the stamp of a personal reminiscence; just as the allusion to the dykes along the coast of Flanders to illustrate those which form the banks of the river Phlegethon, could hardly have occurred to one who had not seen them with his own eyes, though the biographers mention no journey to Flanders. But Sigier's lectures and his life too were over by 1300.

Another little bit of evidence may be given for what it is worth. Any one who has read the discourses of Meister Eckhart, the founder of the school of German mystics, will be struck by the frequent and close resemblances, not of thought only, but of expression and illustration, which exist between him and Dante. So frequent and so close are these, that the reader can hardly conceive the possibility of their being due to mere coincidence.* But Eckhart preached and wrote (if he wrote) in German, a language which we have no reason to think that

* We find close resemblances between Dante and the founder of German mysticism. Not only in similes and illustrations, such as the tailor and his cloth, the needle and the loadstone, the flow of water to the sea, the gravitation of weights to the centre; or in such phrases as Eckhart's "nature possesses nothing swifter than the heaven," or his use of *edilkeit* "nobility," in reference to freewill, *la nobile virtù*. These may have been, in some cases were, borrowed by both from a common source, though the fact of their so often borrowing the same things is suggestive. So, too, both Dante and Eckhart quote St. John i. 3, 4, with the punctuation adopted by Aquinas, *quod factum est, in ipso vita erat* —"what was made, in Him was life"—though the Vulgate and St. Augustine prefer the arrangement of the words familiar to us in our own version. But when we find such an unusual thought as that in *Par.*, viii. 103, 104, of the redeemed soul having no more need to repent of its sins, expressed in almost similar words by Eckhart, it is hardly possible to believe that it occurred to both independently. There are many other instances, but it would occupy too much space if I were to give them here.

Dante knew; so that the exchange of ideas between them, if any, must have taken place by word of mouth, and in French or Latin. Now, Eckhart was for a long time in Paris—so long that he seems to have been known as "Master Eckhart of Paris"—and left that city in 1302. If he and Dante ever met, it must have been in Paris (for though Eckhart went to Italy in 1302, it appears to have been only on a journey to Rome, the last place save Florence where Dante would then have cared to show himself), and that at some time before 1300.

Lastly, we may question if Dante would have chosen Paris as a place of residence while Philip the Fair was on the throne of France.

If, then, he did visit France before his exile, we can date the visit with some certainty. It can hardly have been before 1290, the year of Beatrice's death, nor after 1294, the year in which Carlo Martello came to Florence. Dante's marriage, again, in all probability took place somewhere about the latter year. We know nothing directly of Dante's doings in this interval; nothing, at any rate, inconsistent with his having been for some considerable period away from Florence.

But we have kept till the last the subject which to many is the only one associated with Dante's younger life. What, it will be said, about Beatrice? The fashionable theory nowadays seems to be that there undoubtedly was a lady at Florence of that name, the daughter of Folco Portinari, that she was married to Simone de' Bardi, a member of that great family who were Edward III.'s bankers, and that she died in the flower of her youth. But, say the modern Italian and German writers, this lady—Frau Bardi-Portinari, the latter call her—had no more to do with Dante than any other Beatrice in history. This will seem to many who do not realise on how slight a basis the identification of her rests, to be the very wantonness of paradox. These may be startled to learn that the whole story depends upon the veracity of one man, and that a professed writer of romantic fiction. It is from Boccaccio, and from him alone, that we have learnt to see in Dante's mystical guide and guardian, in the lost love of his early years, only the idealised and allegorised figure of Folco Portinari's daughter. What, then, is his evidence worth? To this we can only reply, that Boccaccio was born eight years before Dante's death; that he lived in Florence from his childhood; that he must have spoken with scores of people to whom the social and literary history of the years preceding 1290 was perfectly familiar; that both Dante and the husband of Beatrice were prominent men; and that Boccaccio can have had no motive for making a statement which, if untrue, he must have known to be so. Further, if the statement had been untrue, it would surely have been contradicted, and some trace of the contradiction would have been found. But, on the contrary, it seems to have been accepted from the first. It is repeated by Boccaccio's younger contemporary and disciple Benvenuto of Imola, who himself lived for some time in Florence, before all those who would be able from their own recollection to confirm or deny it would have passed away. And Benvenuto, it may be noted, though devoted to Boccaccio, was no mere student, but a shrewd and critical man of the world. Dante's son Pietro, indeed, says no word to show that Beatrice was anything but a symbol, and in this some of the other early commentators follow him. But this would prove too much. Whether she be rightly identified with Beatrice Portinari or not, it is impossible for any reader possessing the least knowledge of the human heart to see in the Beatrice of the *Commedia* a symbol merely. Not to mention that it would be quite contrary to Dante's practice thus to *invent* a personage for the sake of the symbol, it is absurd to suppose that the "ten years' thirst" which the sight of her relieves, "the eyes whence Love once took his weapons," and such-like expressions were intended primarily as references to a neglected study of theology or a previous devotion to a contemplative life. The omission, therefore, of the commentators who interested themselves mainly in the allegory to tell us about the real Beatrice cannot be used as evidence against her existence.

The first supporter of what may be called the "superior" view—namely that the whole story of Beatrice is purely allegorical—was one Giovanni Mario Filelfo, a writer of the fifteenth century, born more than a hundred years after Dante's death. As a rule, where his statements can be tested, they are incorrect; and on the whole his work appears to be a mass of unwarranted inferences from unverified assertions. It was not till recent times that his theory on the subject found any defenders.

We may, then, pretty safely continue in the old faith. After all, it explains more difficulties than it raises. No doubt if we cannot free ourselves from modern conceptions we shall be somewhat startled not only by the almost deification of Beatrice, but also by the frank revelation of Dante's passion, with which neither the fact of her having become another man's wife nor his own marriage seems in any way to interfere. It needs, however, but a very slight knowledge of the conditions of life in the thirteenth century to understand the position. As has been already pointed out, the notion of woman's love as a spur to noble living, "the maiden passion for a maid," was quite recent, and at its first growth was quite distinct from the love which finds its fulfilment in marriage. Almost every young man of a literary or intellectual turn seems to have had his Egeria; and when we can identify her she is usually the wife of some one else.

CHAPTER IV.

FLORENTINE AFFAIRS TILL DANTE'S EXILE

In order to understand the extent to which Dante's life was influenced by the political circumstances of his age, it will be well to carry our survey of events somewhat further, with special reference to the affairs of Florence.

As we have seen, after frequent alternations of fortune, the city passed, within two years of Dante's birth, for good and all to the Guelf side. On St. Martin's Day, in November, 1266, Count Guido Novello and his German horse were driven out of the city by the burghers; and though in the January following a treaty of peace was made, and cemented by various marriages between members of the leading families on either side—an arrangement of which the chief result was to embitter party spirit among the Guelfs who had taken no share in it—anything like a lasting reconciliation was soon found to be out of the question. Charles of Anjou, moreover, fresh from his victory over Manfred, was by no means disposed to allow the beaten Ghibelines any chance of rallying. Negotiations were entered into between him and the Florentine Guelfs, and on Easter Day, 1267, Guy of Montfort (son of Sir Simon) entered the city at the head of eight hundred French cavalry. The Ghibelines did not venture to strike a blow, but departed on the day before his arrival. At Easter, says Villani, the crime was committed which first split the city into factions; and at Easter the descendants of the men who had committed the crime went into exile, never to return.

The same year saw a general rally of the north Italian states to the Guelf side, and before many months were out even Lombardy, where, says Villani, there was hardly any memory of the Guelfs, followed the stream. In Tuscany, Pisa and Siena alone held by the tradition—for it was little more—of allegiance to the Empire. The Florentine exiles betook themselves to those cities, and before long the spirits of the party had revived sufficiently to allow them to play what must have been felt to be their last stroke in the game. Profiting by the disaffection of certain Apulian and Sicilian barons (whom one may imagine to have found the gloomy discipline of Charles a poor exchange for the brilliancy and licence of Frederick's Court), they cast their eyes towards the last surviving representative of that Count Frederick who, some two hundred years before, had fixed his seat in the hill-fortress of Staufen. Conrad, or Corradino, as the Italians called him, grandson of Frederick II., was a lad of sixteen, still under the tutelage of his mother, the widow of Conrad IV. Germany seems to have been loyal to him, and had it not been for the impatience of the Italian Ghibelines, he might well have looked forward to regaining, perhaps under more favourable auspices, the Empire which his predecessors had held. But the Tuscan nobles, smarting under defeat, could not wait; and in spite of his mother's opposition, they carried the boy off. Money was lacking; and of the ten thousand German horsemen who accompanied him across the Brenner, only three thousand five hundred went beyond Verona. He passed through

Lombardy, however, without opposition, and with the aid of the Genoese fleet reached Pisa in May, 1268. The rising of the Apulian barons had compelled Charles to return hastily to his kingdom, and Conradin found his way clear to Siena. An action in the district of Arezzo resulted in the defeat and capture of Charles's " marshal," who had come out from Florence in pursuit, and the German force was able to enter Rome unmolested. There they received a reinforcement of eight hundred good Spanish cavalry under Don Henry, brother of the King of Castile, and, elated with success, pushed on to strike a decisive blow. They marched eastward to Tagliacozzo, just within the frontier of the Abruzzi, while Charles reached the same point by forced marches from Nocera. The armies met on St. Bartholomew's Eve, and at first everything seemed to go well for Conradin. The Spanish division defeated the Provençals, and the Germans crushed the French and Italians. But Charles had with him an experienced old knight, Alard de St. Valéry, by whose advice he held a picked force in reserve, concealed behind some rising ground. With this he now attacked the victorious Germans and Spaniards, who had got out of hand in the excitement of pursuit and plundering. They made a bold resistance, but discipline told in the end; they were utterly defeated and their leaders put to flight. Conradin and his immediate staff, comprising the Duke of Austria and some German and Italian nobles, made their way to Astura on the coast of the Campagna, and had succeeded in embarking when they were recognised by one of the Frangipani, who were the lords of the territory. Arrested by him and handed over to Charles, they were subjected to a form of trial, and beheaded in the market-place of Naples. This act has always been regarded as an indelible blot on Charles's record. Dante couples it with the alleged murder, by his order, of St. Thomas Aquinas; and it seems to have been felt even by members of the Guelf party as something, if one may so say, beyond the rules of the game. Pope Clement, according to Villani, blamed Charles severely; and the pious historian, for his own part, sees in the King's subsequent misfortunes the judgment of God upon his cruelty towards an innocent boy. The judge who pronounced the sentence was slain before Charles's very eyes by his son-in-law,

Robert, son to the Count of Flanders, "and not a word was said, for Robert was great with the King, and it appeared to the King and to all the barons that he had acted like a valiant gentleman." In Conradin the Hohenstaufen line came to an end, and therewith all *raison d'être* for the Ghibeline party. After this it became merely a turbulent faction, until the accession of Henry of Luxemburg; when Cæsar once more began to take interest in his Italian dominions.

It may be conceded that party rancour had much more to do with the bringing of Conradin into Italy than any conscientious adhesion to views such as those to which Dante afterwards gave utterance in the *De Monarchia*, or faith in the benefit which would accrue to the world from the rule of a single sovereign. But it shows the hold which the Empire still had on men's minds, that the Ghibeline chiefs should have preferred to take a boy from Germany as the figure-head of their cause, rather than seek a leader of more experience from among their fellow-countrymen. Nor does it seem to have entered any one's mind to look out of Germany for an Emperor. There were, indeed, at the very time, two rival Cæsars-elect in existence—Richard, Earl of Cornwall, and Alfonso, King of Castile, the former of whom his own countrymen, more in derision than respect, were wont to call "King of Almayne;" but clearly no Ghibeline cared to call upon either of them to "heal the wounds which were killing Italy." Later, when the long interregnum was brought to an end by the election of Rudolf of Hapsburg, even the Guelf Villani holds that if he had been willing to pass into Italy he would have been lord of it without opposition; but that astute prince no doubt found himself much better employed in converting a petty baronial line into one of the great houses of Germany, and ultimately of Europe, than in acting up to a titular dignity which brought its bearer more splendour than either wealth or ease. When he did send an Imperial Vicar into Tuscany in 1281 his chance was gone, and the emissary was glad to come to terms with the Florentines.

Thus, from the earliest time that Dante could remember, the Guelfs held an almost undisturbed supremacy throughout Tuscany. There was occasional fighting between Florence, as the head of the Guelf League, and Siena, or Pisa, as the case might be. The Sienese, though helped by Guido Novello and the Florentine exiles, and by some of the Spanish and German troops who had escaped from Tagliacozzo, were badly beaten at Colle di Val d'Elsa in 1269, and their commander, Provenzano Salvani (whom Dante afterwards met in Purgatory), taken and slain. In the following year this city too was purged of the Ghibeline taint, and a few Florentine citizens who were caught were, after a reference to Charles, duly beheaded. Pisa held out somewhat longer, and was able to expel its Guelfs in 1275, among them the famous Count Ugolino de' Gherardeschi, a member of the house of Donoratico, one of whose counts had been captured and killed with Conradin; but in a year's time a Florentine success brought them back. An effort made by Pope Gregory X. to reconcile the factions, as he passed through Florence on his way to the Council of Lyons, bore little or no fruit, and, as a pendant to former excommunications of Emperors, the city was placed under interdict. When, a year and a half later, Gregory died at Arezzo, "by his death," says Villani, "the Guelfs of Florence were greatly cheered, by reason of the ill will which he had towards them;"—an interesting remark, as showing that the Guelfs were not prepared to support the Holy See farther than their own interests as a party demanded.

The condition of Florence at this time cannot be better described than in Villani's words. Writing of the year 1278, he says—

"In these times, the Guelf nobles of Florence, reposing from their foreign wars with victory and honour, and fattened upon the goods of the exiled Ghibelines, and by reason of their other gains, began, through pride and envy, to quarrel among themselves; whence came to pass in Florence more feuds and enmities between the citizens, with slayings and woundings. Among them all the greatest was the quarrel between the house of the Adimari of the one part, who were very great and powerful, and on the other side were the house of the Donati; in such wise that nearly the whole of the city took sides, and some held with one party and some with the other, whereby the city and the Guelf party were in great danger."

We shall remember how, in Dante's judgement also, pride, envy, and avarice were "the sparks that had set hearts on fire," in Florence.

Once again the Pope, who was now Nicholas III., interfered; and once again representatives of the two great factions exchanged the kiss of peace before a Papal Legate, this time in front of "the Preaching Friars' new church of New St. Mary's, in Florence," of which the Legate, Cardinal Latino, had but lately laid the first stone. The Ghibeline leaders were still kept out, but the rank and file returned. The feud of the Adimari and Donati was patched up for the time, whereby "the said Cardinal had much honour, and Florence remained a good time in a peaceful and good and tranquil state."

Cardinal Latino had arranged for the government of Florence by a committee of fourteen "good men," of whom eight were to be Guelfs and six Ghibelines. They were to hold office for two months. It marks the Cardinal as a man of some organizing capacity that his peace continued for four years, during which time Villani has next to nothing to relate about the affairs of his city. These were the years in which Dante was growing up to manhood. As a boy of thirteen he would doubtless have looked on at the scene in front of Santa Maria Novella; and during the next four peaceful years we may suppose that he would have begun to sit at the feet of the old statesman, diplomatist, and scholar Brunetto Latini, picking up from his lips the lore "how man becomes immortal." We can picture him too, where the boys and girls were gathered together, a silent and reserved lad, probably unpopular unless with one or two special friends, paying little heed to any of his companions save one girl of about his own age, whose movements he would follow, and for the sound of whose words, though never addressed to him, he would listen, with the speechless devotion which perhaps is only felt at sixteen or seventeen, and then only by natures which fortunately are exceptional in this world. "The child is father to the man;" and we can be pretty certain from what we know of the man Dante what the boy Dante must have been.

The tranquil period was disturbed in 1282. Pope Nicholas, who, whether guilty of Simony or not—and one fears that the case against him must have been strong, since not only Dante, but even Villani charges him with the offence—at least deserved the blessing pronounced on peacemakers, had died in the previous year at Viterbo, a town which, during this period, seems to have suited the Popes better than Rome as a place of residence. Charles, between whom and Nicholas no love had been lost, was resolved that the next Pope should not come from the powerful house of the Orsini, to a branch of which, the Guatani, the late Pontiff had belonged, and by an arrangement with the people of Viterbo, succeeded in getting the two most prominent clerical members of that house imprisoned. Thus he secured the election of a Frenchman, Simon of Brie, who, being a canon of Tours, took the name of Martin IV. His Papacy, though it lasted little more than three years, was eventful. He was elected in January, 1282, and on the following Easter Monday, March 30th, the people of Palermo, furious at the outrages of Charles's French troops, rose and massacred every Frenchman upon whom they could lay hands. Charles's efforts to re-capture the island were baffled, chiefly owing to the hostility of Manfred's son-in-law. King Peter of Aragon, also, with the help of his famous admiral, Roger of Loria, began about this time to prove a serious thorn in the side of the Angevin King. From the day of the "Sicilian Vespers," fortune turned against Charles. His son was taken prisoner by Loria in 1284, his life being spared only at the entreaty of Peter's wife, while he did not recover his liberty till 1289. The King himself died broken down with grief and disappointment, in the early days of 1285, and was followed a couple of months later by his creature, Martin IV., and, before the year was out, by his enemy, King Peter. It will be remembered that Peter and Charles were seen by Dante in the "Valley of Princes," awaiting their entry into Purgatory, and singing their Compline hymn in friendly accord: Martin IV. being placed higher up the mountain, among the gluttonous.

At Florence the course of affairs was not much affected by the reverses which befell Charles. At the same time, these, and a success gained by Guy of Montefeltro over John of Appia, a French officer whom Martin had appointed Count of Romagna, made the Guelf majority uneasy. Cardinal Latino's Constitution was abandoned, and a new form of government adopted. The trading-class resolved to get rid altogether of the representatives of feudal authority, weak as they had become,* and to this

* In 1300, when the Black and White factions arose, we find among the twenty-eight houses enumerated by Machiavelli, as

end the Fourteen were abolished, and the chief power placed in the hands of the Priors of the Arts, or, as we should say, the Masters of the great trading guilds. The number of those guilds which contributed members to the governing body seems to have been gradually increased. At first only three—the Clothmakers, the Money-changers, and the Wool-dealers—were thus honoured; but by the end of the century, at least twelve, seven greater and five lesser arts, were included. The Priors, as the Fourteen had done, held office for two months only, and various devices were employed to prevent any house or any person from becoming dangerously powerful. Nobles, in order to qualify for office, had to join a guild; and as the nobles, or *grandi*, were more frequently on the Ghibeline side, this would yet further weaken that party.

Florence had now fairly entered upon a period of great prosperity. Her bankers lent money to kings; her trade extended all over Europe. Pisa, her most dangerous rival, had been utterly crushed by the Genoese in the great sea-fight off Meloria,

the chief on either side, only *three* which in the old days had belonged to the Ghibeline party.

with a slaughter which seems to have struck awe into the hearts even of the victors; and though she expelled her Guelfs four years later, in 1288, and, in 1291, under the brilliant leader Guy of Montefeltro, won some successes in the field, she was never again a power to be feared. Arezzo gave some trouble as a rendezvous for the banished Ghibelines; but the battle of Campaldino, in 1289, already referred to, broke her strength for a long time. Florence was thus free to attend to the arts of peace. The city walls were extended and new gates built; and several of the buildings, which to this day are among the glories of Florence, date from that period. Still, however, much of the old class-jealousy smouldered; and, as Machiavelli points out, all fear of the Ghibelines being removed, the powerful houses began to oppress the people. Giano della Bella, himself of noble family, casting in his lot with the commons, succeeded in carrying what were called the Ordinances of Justice, whereby, among other things, nobles were absolutely disqualified from taking any part in the government. A measure so oppressive as this was bound to bring about its own appeal, and, as a matter of fact, within two years from its promulgation, Giano was driven into exile, and the nobles were more turbulent than ever. It is at this time that the name of Corso Donati first comes into prominence.

Another event, which was to influence the destinies of Florence and of Dante, occurred shortly before Giano's overthrow. This was the election to the Papacy, in 1294, of Benedetto Guatani, known to history as Boniface VIII. The most vigorous Pope who had held the office for several generations, he soon let it be known that he intended to revive all the claims which his predecessors, Gregory VII. and Innocent III., had made to temporal as well as spiritual supremacy. His first efforts were devoted to getting Tuscany into his hands, and to this end he seems to have intrigued freely with the leaders of both parties in Florence. In theory, of course, where all were Guelfs, the Pope ought to have had little trouble; but there were Guelfs and Guelfs, and it was not long before party differences were emphasised, and, so to say, crystallised, by party names. Curiously enough, these again appear first at Pistoia. A family feud there had led to two branches of the Cancellieri being distinguished as Black and White, and towards 1300 the names appear at Florence. The Donati headed the Black faction; their rivals, the Cerchi, the White. The latter represented the more orderly section of the community; the former reproduced all the worst features of the old Ghibeline aristocracy, though in the end it was the Whites who had to coalesce with the Ghibelines. At first, indeed, it would seem as if Boniface might have been willing to work with the Whites. He sent for Vieri de' Cerchi, the leader of that party, and tried to induce him to live peaceably with the other side. Vieri, for reasons which we can only conjecture, replied curtly that he had no quarrel with any one; and Boniface resorted to the old expedient of sending a Cardinal — Matthew of Acquasparta—to reconcile the factions.

We have now reached the critical year of Dante's life—that in which he held the office of Prior. But for the events of this and the next two years, it may be doubted whether the *Commedia* would ever have come into existence, at least in the form in which six centuries have studied and admired it. Henceforth Dante's own history, rather than that of his times, will be our chief subject.

CHAPTER V.

DANTE'S EXILE

Towards the end of the thirteenth century, Dante's name begins to appear in public documents as taking a share in the business of the State. Thus he spoke in the "Council of the Hundred" on December 10, 1296, and in the following March, in opposition, it would seem, to a proposal of a grant to King Charles II. of Apulia. In May, 1299, he acted as ambassador from Florence to the neighbouring city of San Gemignano, the only one of all the numerous embassies ascribed to him by some biographers in which modern criticism will still allow us to believe. Finally, in 1300, probably from June 15th to August 15th, he served his term as Prior.

The Constitution of Florence at this time was somewhat complicated. It will be sufficient to say here that the government was carried on by a committee of six priors, who held office for two months only; and that in order to be eligible for the offices of State a man had to be enrolled in one of the twelve trading guilds known as Arts, of which seven ranked as "greater," five as "less." Dante belonged to one of the "greater arts," that of the *speziali*, "dealers in spices," which included the apothecaries and, as it is believed, the booksellers. The number of priors was so large, and their tenure of office so short, that the selection of any particular citizen would hardly imply more than that he was regarded as a man of good business capacity; but in 1300 public affairs in Florence were in such a critical state, that one may well suppose the citizens to have been especially careful in their choice. In the previous April an accusation had been brought by Lapo Salterelli (afterwards one of Dante's fellow-exiles, not held by him in much esteem), who then was Prior, against three citizens of Florence—Simon Gherardi, Noffo Quintavalle, and Cambio, son of Sesto, of conspiring against the State. The facts are somewhat obscure, but, as it appears that they were all connected with the Papal Court, and that Boniface made strong efforts to get the fine imposed on them remitted, we may conjecture that they had in some way abetted his scheme of "getting Tuscany into his hands." In a remarkable letter addressed to the Bishop of Florence, in which a good deal of the argument, and even some of the language, of Dante's *De Monarchia* is curiously paralleled, of course from the opposite point of view, the Pope requires the attendance before him of Lapo (whom he styles *vere lapis offensionis*) and the other accusers. As may be supposed, no notice was taken of this requisition, and the fines were duly enforced.

Boniface's letter is dated from Anagni, on May 15th. Before it was written, the first actual bloodshed in the feud between the Black and White parties had taken place. Some of the young Donati and Cerchi, with their respective friends, were in the Piazza di Santa Trinità on May 1st, looking on at a dance. Taunts were exchanged, blows followed, and "Ricoverino, son of Messer Ricovero de' Cerchi, by misadventure got his nose cut off his face." The leading Guelfs, seeing what a chance the split in their party would offer to the Ghibelines, sought the mediation of the Pope. Boniface was of course willing enough to interfere, and, as has been said, sent Matthew of Acquasparta, Cardinal of Ostia, a former General of the Franciscans, to Florence as peacemaker. He arrived just about the time when the new Priors, including, as we must suppose, Dante, were entering on office, and was received with great honour. But when it came to measures of pacification, he seems to have had nothing better to suggest than the selection of the Priors by lot, in place of their nomination (as had hitherto been the custom) by their predecessors and the chiefs of the guilds. "Those of the White party," says Villani, "who controlled the government of the country, through fear of losing their position, and of being hoodwinked by the Pope and the Legate through the reform aforesaid, took the worser counsel, and would not obey." So the familiar interdict was launched once more, and the Legate departed.

In the city, things went from bad to worse. At the funeral of a lady belonging to the Frescobaldi, a White family, in the following December, a bad brawl arose, in which the Cerchi had the worst of it. But when the Donati, emboldened by this success, attacked their rivals on the highway, the Commune took notice of it, and the assailants were imprisoned, in default of paying their fines. Some of the Cerchi were also fined, and, though able to pay, went to prison, apparently from motives of economy, contrary to Vieri's advice. Unluckily for them, the governor of the prison, one of their own faction, " an accursed Ser Neri degli Abati," a scion of a family which seems, if we may trust Dante's mention of some of its other members, to have made a "speciality" of treacherous behaviour, introduced into the prison fare a poisoned millet-pudding, whereof two of the Cerchi died, and two of the opposite party as well,* "and no blood-feud came about for that" —probably because it was felt that the score was equal.

The Blacks now made a move. The "captains of the Guelf party," who, though holding no official position, seem to have exercised a sort of *imperium in imperio*, were on their side; and a meeting was held in Holy Trinity Church, at which it was resolved to send a deputation to Boniface, requesting him to take once again what seems to us—and

---

* So I understand an obviously corrupt passage in Villani, viii. 41. One of the unlucky Blacks was a Portinari, doubtless a kinsman of Beatrice—a fact which curiously seems to have escaped the conjectural commentators.

indeed was—the fatal step of calling in French aid. The stern prophecy which Dante puts into the mouth of Hugh Capet in Purgatory was to be fulfilled:—

> "I see the time at hand
> That forth from France invites another Charles
> To make himself and kindred better known.
> Unarm'd he issues, saving with that lance
> Which the arch-traitor tilted with; and that
> He carries with so home a thrust, as rives
> The bowels of poor Florence."

We may probably date from this Dante's final severance from the Guelf party; and, at any rate, we may judge from it the real value of Guelf patriotism.

It must be remembered that the Black faction was still but a faction. The conspiracy leaked out, and popular indignation was aroused. The *Signoria* that is, the Priors, took action. Corso Donati and the other leaders were heavily fined, and this time the fines were paid. Probably they did not wish to taste Ser Neri degli Abati's cookery a second time. A good many of the junior members of the party were banished to Castello della Pieve; and at the same time, "to remove all jealousy," several of the White leaders were sent to Serezzano (which we now call Sarzana)—a weak and unlucky attempt at compromise. They were, indeed, soon allowed to return, their place of exile being unhealthy; so much so that one of them, Dante's most intimate friend, Guido Cavalcanti, died in the course of the winter from illness contracted there.

Cardinal Matthew seems not to have actually left Florence till after the beginning of 1301. We are told that among his other demands (probably made on this occasion), was one to the effect that Florence should furnish a hundred men-at-arms for the Pope's service; and that Dante, who, after his term of office as Prior, remained a member of the council, moved that nothing should be done in the matter. Indeed, in the scanty notices which we have of his doings in this critical period, he appears as the steady opponent of all outside interference in the affairs of Florence, whether by Pope or Frenchman. In the face of this it is hard to understand how the famous story of his having gone on an embassy to Rome—" If I stay, who goes? If I go, who stays?"—can ever have obtained credence. Some words like those he may well have used, in the magnificent self-consciousness which elsewhere made him boast of having formed a party by himself; but we cannot suppose that he would at any time in the course of 1301 have thus put his head into the lion's mouth. That Boniface was at the time of the supposed mission not at Rome but at Anagni is a minor detail.

If all the White party had possessed Dante's energy, Florence might have been saved. Vieri de' Cerchi had, indeed, as we have seen, spirit enough to tell the Pope in effect to mind his own business, and he was not devoid of shrewdness; but he seems to have been incapable of any sustained vigour in action. The party as a whole were probably as corrupt as their rivals, and less astute—"an evil and foolish company," as Dante afterwards called them by the mouth of Cacciaguida. Corso Donati, on the other hand, was a bold and reckless intriguer. He followed up the conspiracy of the Santa Trinità by hastening to the Papal Court, and inducing Boniface to send at once for Charles of Valois, brother of the French king, Philip the Fair. Charles obeyed the summons readily, in the hope, says Villani, of the Imperial crown. After a visit to the Pope at Anagni, he entered Florence on All Saints' Day, 1301. All opposition on the part of the Whites was disarmed by the assurance that he came only as "peacemaker;" and a meeting, "at which I, the writer, was present," was held in the Church of Santa Maria Novella. Charles, "with his own mouth, undertook and swore, and promised as a King's son to maintain the city in peace and good estate; and incontinently by him and by his people the contrary was done." Armed men were introduced; Corso Donati, though under sentence of banishment, entered with them, Vieri de' Cerchi, in foolish confidence, forbidding his arrest. The populace, promptly seeing who were the masters, raised a shout of "Long live Lord Charles and the Baron" (the name given to Corso); and the city was given up for a week to burning and pillage. A second visit from the Cardinal of Acquasparta produced no result, save a momentary truce and another interdict. Throughout the early months of 1302, killings and slayings went on, Corso's only son, among others, being mortally wounded in the act of murdering one of the Cerchi. Finally, one of the French knights, acting in the capacity which to this day is regarded as peculiarly suited to the French genius, that of *agent provocateur*, induced some of the White party, by offers of help, to form some kind of conspiracy against Charles's person. This plot being duly reported, the conspirators fled on April 4th, some to Pisa, some to Arezzo, some to Pistoia, and joined the already exiled Ghibelines. They were condemned as rebels, and their houses destroyed. From this time the Whites and Ghibelines form one party.

Whether Dante actually went with them is a perplexing question which has never been thoroughly solved, but is of sufficient interest to delay us for a while. In the short biography of the poet which Villani gives when recording his death, we read: "This Dante was a citizen of Florence, honourable and of old family, belonging to the ward of St. Peter's Gate, and a neighbour of ours. His exile from Florence was for the reason that when Lord Charles of Valois, of the house of France, came to Florence in 1301 and drove out the White party, as is mentioned above under the date, the said Dante was one of the chief governors of our city, and belonged to that party, Guelf though he was; and therefore, *for no other fault*, he was driven forth and banished with the said White party from Florence." This seems very explicit, but there are difficulties in the way of taking it quite literally. A document exists, dated January 27, 1302, in which the Podestà, Cante de' Gabrielli of Gubbio, charges Dante Alighieri and three others with various offences, the chief being *baratteria* (or corrupt jobbery in office), the use of public money to resist the entrance of Charles of Valois, and interference in the affairs of Pistoia with the view of securing the expulsion from that city "of those who are called Blacks, faithful, men devoted to the Holy Roman Church," which had taken place in May, 1301. It is stated that, having been duly summoned, they had contumaciously absented themselves, which seems to show that they were not in Florence; and they are sentenced to pay five thousand florins apiece within three days, or, in default, be banished and have their houses destroyed and their goods confiscated; and in any case they were banished for two years. A second decree of March 10th condemns Dante and fourteen others, among them Lapo Salterelli, if they fall into the power of the Commonwealth, to be burnt to death.

As has been said, Dante must clearly have been out of Florence when this document was launched. Leonardi Bruni says he was at Rome on an embassy when the Whites left Florence, and that he hastened to join his party at Siena; but for the reasons already given, this story of the embassy cannot be accepted. Some have suggested that as at Florence the old style prevailed, under which March 26th was New Year's Day, the two sentences really belong to what we should now call 1303, when Dante had undoubtedly been in exile for some months, and this is corroborated by Benvenuto's statement, "bannitus fuit anno MCCCIII."—"bannitus" meaning, no doubt, "placed under ban," as distinct from voluntary exile. But it appears that Cante de' Gabrielli went out of office in June, 1302. So, unless we can suppose this last date to be wrong—and there is some little ground for suspecting it—we must assume that, though a

Florentine official, he did not use Florentine style, and that Dante, with some few others of the leading White Guelfs, was compelled to fly sooner than the bulk of his party. He may very well have been regarded as a specially dangerous opponent.

That there was any foundation for the charge of corruption it is impossible to believe. Dante's faults were many, but they did not lie in that direction; and the honest Villani, though he appears to have sided with the Black party, and indeed held office himself as Prior only a few years later, seems to have introduced the words which we have italicised in the passage given above, with the express intention of indicating this. On the other hand, it may be noted that the charge was ingeniously devised. Dante is known to have been in debt, for some of his notes-of-hand exist, belonging to the years preceding 1300; while in the course of 1301 he was engaged in superintending the performance of certain public works in the city. Thus it would be matter of common knowledge both that he was short of money and that he had recently been in a position offering good opportunities for peculation, a fact of which his unscrupulous adversaries would naturally avail themselves. We may perhaps see, in the large space which he devotes, in the *Hell*, to the crime of *baratteria*, evidence of a wish to express his especial detestation of it.

What, however, we know for certain is that, after some date early in the year 1302, Dante never saw Florence again. Several attempts were made by the exiles to win their way back, but they were uniformly unsuccessful, and only led to fresh sentences against those who took part in them. Whether Dante was among these, at all events during the earlier years of his exile, seems very doubtful. We know from his own words that he had no sympathy with the men with whom he was thrown. Indeed, it was a curious irony of fate which linked in one condemnation his name and that of Lapo Salterelli, a man whom he selects (*Par.*, xv. 128) as an example of the degradation into which the Florentine character had fallen. During this first period he was probably eating his heart, and watching for the coming of the deliverer who, by bringing all the world under one impartial sway, should put an end to faction and self-seeking—the *invidia* and *avarizia* against which he is for ever inveighing—and permit every man "to sit at ease and perfect himself in prudence and wisdom;" thus fulfilling his proper task of "making himself immortal," or, as St. Paul phrases it, coming "to the measure of the stature of the fulness of Christ." It is a noble conception, though the six hundred years which have elapsed since Dante looked for its fulfilment do not seem to have brought us very much more forward in that direction. Still, we can give him the honour due to a lofty standard of political and social conduct in a violent and profligate, if brilliant, age; and we can still read with interest and profit that wonderful repertory of political wisdom, dialectical argument (after the manner of the schoolmen), and passionate pleading for good government, which he calls the *Treatise on Monarchy*.

The date at which the *De Monarchia* was composed is uncertain, but it would seem to belong most fitly to the years which immediately succeeded Dante's banishment. The Empire was in the hands of the incapable Albert of Hapsburg, while the Pope, from 1305, was the creature of the French King. Cæsar and Peter seemed both alike to have abdicated, and the world was going from bad to worse. With the election of Henry of Luxemburg, in 1308, better times may seem to have dawned, when practice might supersede abstract theories. The letter which Dante actually wrote to Henry in 1311 is couched in a far less meditative tone.

During Henry's short reign the Ghibeline cause looked up; nor was his death in 1313 so fatal a blow to it as might have been expected. Several powerful leaders arose, one of whom, Uguccione della Faggiuola of Pisa, won back most of Tuscany for his party. In 1315 he inflicted a severe defeat on the Florentines and their allies at Montecatini, on the border of the Florentine and Lucchese territories; but he was unable to follow up his success so far as to enter the city. Some two months later a third sentence went forth against Dante, in which his sons were included, condemning them, as Ghibelines and rebels against the Commonwealth and people of Florence and the statutes of the Guelf party, to be beheaded whenever taken. It has been plausibly suggested that the two events were not unconnected; and as it is hardly likely that at the age of fifty Dante would have taken a prominent part in the actual fighting, we must suppose it to have been as a leading adviser of the enemy that he was specially obnoxious to the ruling powers at Florence.

The chief importance, however, which Dante's exile has for us, is that with it his great literary activity began. He had, of course, written all his life; and it is quite possible even that some portion of the *Commedia* had been composed before he left Florence. The story told by Boccaccio is well known. Commenting upon the opening words of Canto viii., he tells us that the preceding portion of the poem had been written before the final catastrophe, and left behind by Dante in his flight, not being discovered for some years. In any case, the *Vita Nuova* was written, as he himself tells us, before he was twenty-five; and a good deal of the *Convito*, a work which looks very much as if it had first come into existence as the contents of notebooks, in which materials to be afterwards worked into the great poem were jotted down, was no doubt in writing. But it is to Dante's twenty years of exile that we owe in their completed form the works which place him not only among the world's five or six greatest poets, but in an eminent position among philosophers, theologians, statesmen, and men of science.

We have but little certain information as to Dante's life during his exile. Legends innumerable have sprung up as to his residence here, there, and elsewhere; but most of these are based on the fancies of later writers; or in some cases even on local vanity, which was flattered by the remotest connection with the great name. We can say for certain that he passed some time at Verona, some at Lucca, some at Ravenna, where his sepulchre remains to this day; and with some approach to probability we can place him at Paris, at Bologna, and perhaps at Milan. He may possibly have spent some time in the Lunigiana, and some in the Casentino. All we know is that his life was spent in wandering, that he had no settled home, that he lived on other men's bread, and went up and down other men's stairs. He was honoured, it is true. Great nobles were glad to employ his services, and, as we have said, the fact of his being so often selected by the rulers of Florence for condemnation, shows that at least they regarded him as a man to be reckoned with. But probably the strongest evidence of the estimation in which he was held is to be found in Villani's obituary chapter, wherein his character and accomplishments are set forth with a fulness which the historian elsewhere reserves for Popes and sovereigns; a fulness all the more noteworthy since his name never occurs in the chronicle of events in which he undoubtedly took a leading part.

Only when Italy and Florence had lost him beyond hope of recovery was it realised that he was one of his country's greatest glories. Then chairs were founded from which the most eminent literary men of the age should expound his works; and commentator after commentator—nine or ten before the end of the fourteenth century—cleared up some obscurities and made others more obscure. Of course, so far as historical allusions go, the writers who were nearly or quite contemporary with the events are often of great service; but it is otherwise, as a rule, when a knowledge of books is wanted. We are never so much impressed with the vastness of Dante's reading, as when we see the utter failure of these learned men even to observe, in many cases, that any explanation or illustration of an allusion is wanted. This, however, brings us back to the point from which we started, namely, that much as has been written about Dante, the possible fields of research are by no means exhausted.

The interest of the events which moulded Dante's career and influenced his work has perhaps led to their occupying too large a share of these pages; but it has been thought best to go into the history at some length, as being after all the first and most essential step towards a thorough comprehension of the position which his writings, and especially the *Commedia*, hold in European literature. This is quite unique of its kind. Never before or since has a poem of the highest imagination served—not merely as a political manifesto, but—as a party pamphlet; and we may safely say that no such poem will in future serve that purpose, at all events until the conditions under which it was produced occur. Whether that is ever likely to be the case, those who have followed the history may judge.

CHAPTER VI.

THE "COMMEDIA"

So many good summaries of the *Commedia* exist that to give another may appear superfluous. At the same time, experience shows not only that such a summary is found by most readers to be the best of all helps to the study of the poem, but also that every fresh summariser treats it from a somewhat different point of view. It is therefore possible that in the following pages answers, or at least suggestions of answers, may be found to some questions which previous writers, in England at all events, have passed over; and that they may serve in some measure as a supplement to the works which will be mentioned in the appendix.

§ 1. HELL.

The first eleven cantos of the *Hell* form a very distinct subdivision of the poem. They embrace, first, the introduction contained in Canto i.; secondly, the description of the place of punishment up to a point at which a marked change in the character of the sins punished is indicated. In one sense, no doubt, an important stage in the journey is completed when the City of Dis is reached, in Canto viii.; but it will be observed, when we reach that point, that the class of sinners who are met with immediately within the walls of the City, the Epicureans or, as we should now say, the Materialists, bear really a much stronger affinity to those who are outside the walls, those whose sin has been lack of self-restraint in one form or another, than they do to the worse criminals who have "offended of malicious wickedness," and who lie at and below the foot of the steep guarded by the Minotaur. The former class at all events have been, to use a common phrase, "their own worst enemies;" their sins have not been, at any rate in their essence, like those of the latter, of the kind which break up the fabric of society, and with them the heretics may most naturally be considered. It can hardly be doubted that some such view as this led Dante to make the first great break of level in his scheme of the lower world at a point which would leave the freethinkers and materialists actually nearer to the sinners of whom he holds that their sin "men Dio offende," even though theological exigencies compel him to place them within the walls of the "red-hot city." We may thus conveniently take these eleven cantos for consideration as a group by themselves.

In the earlier cantos, as indeed throughout the poem, the main difficulties with which we meet depend far more on interpretation than on the mere "construing" of the words; and even if it were otherwise, all purely linguistic difficulties have been so fully dealt with over and over again in commentaries and translations that it would, as has been said, be quite superfluous to enter here upon any discussion of them. The opening canto, as every reader will at once perceive, is symbolism and allegory from beginning to end, from the "dark wood" in which the action of the poem begins to the "hound" who is to free Italy. These, more especially the latter, have given as much trouble to the interpreter as anything in the whole poem; indeed it may be said that in the matter of the *Veltro* we have not made much advance on

Boccaccio, who frankly admitted that he could not tell what was meant. But between these two points we have some hundred lines in nearly every one of which, beside its obvious and literal interpretation, we must look for all the others enumerated by Dante in the famous passage of his letter to Can Grande. The second canto is of much the same character, in some respects almost in more need of close study. The significance of the three beasts who hinder Dante is easier to make out than that of the three heavenly ladies who assist him. Meantime, if we are content to read the poem as narrative merely, there is no great difficulty to be overcome. The language is straightforward on the whole, almost the only *crux* being ii. 108, which has not yet been satisfactorily explained, nor is the imagery other than simple.

With Canto iii. and the arrival within the actual portal of Hell (though hardly in Hell properly so called) we enter upon a fresh subdivision of the poem; and are very soon brought up by the first, and one of the most perplexing, of the allusions to contemporary history with which it abounds. The elucidation of these would constantly offer almost hopeless difficulties, were it not for the early commentators, who are often able to explain them from personal knowledge. Now and then, however, it happens that they differ, and then the modern student is at a loss. This has been in some measure the case with the famous "gran rifiuto," iii. 60; so that while we may with a high degree of probability accept the more usual view that the allusion is to the abdication of Celestine V., we cannot without further evidence feel so certain about it as we could wish. The whole conception of this canto seems to be due to Dante's own invention; only to a nature like his, keenly alive to the eternal distinction between right and wrong, and burning with zeal in the cause of right, could it have occurred to mark off for special ignominy people whose sole fault seems to have been that they "took things too easily." When, in Canto iv., we pass the river of Acheron, and find ourselves for the first time actually on the border of Hell itself, we are conscious at first of an alleviation. Melancholy there is, but it is a dignified melancholy, as different from the sordid misery of the wretches we have just left, as the "noble city" and the green sward enclosed by it are different from the murky air and the foul mud among which they have to dwell. Both in this and in the second circle we have punishment indeed but without degradation, even with some mitigation. Virgil at least enjoys the converse of the sages and great men of old and, in so far as non-Christians go, of recent times; while Francesca is solaced by the perpetual companionship of him for whose sake she has lost her soul. Even the penalty which she suffers, of being whirled for ever on the storm, is not exactly humiliating. From this point, however, we are conscious of a change. The gluttons seated or lying on putrid earth and exposed to lashing rain; the misusers of wealth, with all human lineaments effaced, and engaged in a foolish and wearisome scuffle; the ill-tempered, floating on the surface of the foul marsh of Styx or lying submerged in it according as their disposition was to fierce wrath or sullen brooding—all these are not merely tormented but degraded as well.

After crossing the Styx (Canto viii.) we find a further change. Thus far the sins punished have differed only in degree from those which we shall find being expiated in Purgatory. They are indeed the simpler forms, so to speak, of the defects common to all animal nature. They are the same which, in one of their interpretations, the three symbolical beasts of Canto i. denote. Henceforth we find sins which are only possible to the higher intelligence of humanity. It will be observed, too, that at this point what may be called pictorial description begins. Hitherto we have had merely a general impression of murky air and miry soil, sloping perhaps a little toward the centre, and intersected now and again by a stream. Now the City of Dis with minarets and towers rises in front of us, and, as we shall see in future cantos, from this time onwards the character of the scenery is indicated with great preciseness, even to its smallest details. Here, too, actual devils, beings whose will, as Aquinas says, is obstinately set upon evil, appear for the first time, as distinct from the personages of classical mythology, who act as warders of the various circles. Virgil, or human reason, is no longer sufficient of himself to secure a passage. Both at the gates of the fiery city and on subsequent occasions he is as helpless, without superior aid, as his disciple and follower.

The ninth canto contains a piece of allegory, that involved in the introduction of Medusa and the Furies, which has earned perhaps a greater reputation for obscurity than it deserves, from the fact that Dante himself calls special attention to it.

Cantos x. and xi. are both very important, the former for its bearing on the history of Florence. Those who have read the sketch of that history in the preceding chapters will understand the full force of Farinata's discourse with Dante. We have had a brief passage of the same kind in Canto vi., but here the subject is treated at greater length, and with some marvellous dramatic touches.

Canto xi. must be thoroughly mastered if Dante's scheme of ethics is to be understood. It forms, indeed, a summary of and key to the arrangement of the penalties, and a thorough comprehension and retention of it in the memory will be found a wonderful help to a recollection of the whole Cantica.

At the conclusion of the discourse in which Dante, speaking by the mouth of Virgil, has set forth this ethical system, the poets move forward along the brink of the pit until they arrive at a spot where they can reach the lower level. The descent is rendered possible by a steep and broken slope of loose rock, which Dante compares to the great landslip between Trent and Verona, known as the Slavino di Marco.* Virgil explains that this was due to the "rending of the rocks" at the time of the Crucifixion. The descent is guarded by the legendary Minotaur, the Cretan monster, part bull, part man. In this connection it may be noticed that the beings suggested by classical mythology, who are met with in the division of Hell which lies between the wall of the City of Dis and the brink of Malebolge, the Minotaur, the Centaurs, the Harpies, and Geryon (as Dante conceives him), all belong to the semi-bestial class. In spite of the opinion held by some of the most eminent Dante-scholars, that Dante in his classification of sins does not follow Aristotle's grouping of them into incontinent, malicious, and brutal, but recognises the first two only, it seems difficult not to see in this, especially when it is taken in connection with expressions scattered throughout his

* Not only this allusion, but the occurrence, in this and other parts of the poem, of several words used in that district makes it almost certain that Dante was very familiar with the country round about Trent. Doubtless he would visit it from Verona.

writings, an indication that in the sins of the seventh circle he found the equivalent of the Greek philosopher's θηριότης—the result of giving a free range to the brutal, as distinct from the common animal, impulses.

In this seventh circle, too, we first meet with *fire* as an instrument of Divine wrath. Indeed, with the single exception of the suicides, for whom a specially significant chastisement is devised, all the sinners in this group, from the heretics in their red-hot tombs to the usurers tormented on one side by the fiery rain, and on the other by the exhalations from the deeper pit, are punished by means of heat. At the foot of the slope is a great circular plain, ringed with a river of boiling blood in which spoilers, robbers, and murderers, some famous, some obscure, are plunged more or less deeply in proportion to the heinousness of their crimes; for, like earthly streams, this has its deep and shallow. At the latter point they cross, on the back of Nessus the Centaur, and at once enter (Canto xiii.) a wood of gnarled and sere trees, in which the Harpies have their dwelling. These trees have sprung from the souls of suicides, and retain the power of speech and sensation. From one of these, who in life had been the famous statesman Peter de Vincis, Dante learns that at the judgement they will recover their bodies, like others, but will not be allowed to reassume them. The body will be hung on the tree to which it belongs. Here, as in the case of the avaricious and the wrathful, the spirits of other sinners take a part in the infliction of the punishment. The wood is inhabited by the souls of those who had wasted their substance in life, and these are constantly chased through it by hounds, with much destruction of leaves and twigs.

On issuing from the wood (Canto xiv.), they find themselves at the edge of a great circular plain of sand, upon which flakes of fire are ceaselessly dropping. Skirting the wood for some distance they reach the bank of the stream of blood which, having circled all round the outer margin of the wood, now comes flowing through it, and crosses the sandy plain in a channel carefully built of shaped stone. Virgil takes occasion to explain the origin of the rivers of Hell. Thick fumes rise from it which quench the falling flames, so that along its bank, and there only, can a way be found. As they proceed they find sinners lying prone or running under the fiery shower. These are they who had done violence to God, either directly by open blasphemy, or indirectly by violating the divinely appointed natural order whereby both the race of mankind and its possessions should increase and multiply. Many famous Florentines are among these sinners (Cantos xv. and xvi.); and Dante talks long with the famous statesman and philosopher, Brunetto Latini, who had been his early friend and adviser, and with sundry great captains and men of renown. After this they reach the point where the river falls with a mighty roar down to the next level. There is no natural means of descent here available; and Dante hands to Virgil a cord with which he is girt. The meaning of this cord is very obscure. He says: "I once thought to capture the leopard with it;" and if the leopard denotes the factions of Florence, the cord may perhaps symbolise justice or equity. When Virgil has thrown it down they wait a short time, and presently a monster appears whose name we find to be Geryon, and who symbolises fraud or treachery. It is perhaps not unnatural that when the power to enforce justice has been cast away, treachery should raise its head. This monster draws near the brink (Canto xvii.), but before they mount on him, Virgil allows Dante to walk a few paces to the right, in order that he may take note of the last class of "violent" sinners, namely, the usurers. These hold an intermediate position between the violent and the treacherous; just as the heretics did between the incontinent and the violent. Here again are many Florentines. Like the other misusers of money in Canto vii. their features are unrecognisable, and they are only to be known by the arms embroidered on their money bags. After hearing a few words from one of them, Dante returns to Virgil, and both take their place on the croup of Geryon, who bears them downwards to the eighth circle. This (Canto xviii.), from its configuration, is known as Malebolge, or Evilpits. It is divided into ten concentric rings, or circular trenches, separated by a tract of rocky ground. From various indications we gather that each trench is half a mile across, and the intervening ground a mile and a quarter. The trenches are spanned by rocky ribs, forming bridges by which the central cavity can be reached. Here we find for the first time devils, in the ordinary acceptation of the term, employed as tormentors. The sinners in this circle are those who have been guilty in any way of leading others into sin, deceiving or cheating them, without any aggravating circumstances of ingratitude or breach of natural ties. In the first pit are those who have led women astray; these are scourged by fiends. In the next lie flatterers immersed in the most loathsome filth. In each Dante notes two examples: one of recent times—indeed, in both cases an acquaintance of his own,—and one taken from ancient history or legend. Jason, for his desertion of Hypsipyle and Medea, is the classical example of the first offence. Of this use of mythological persons we have many examples, but the typical flatterer of old time is a more curious selection, being a character in a play, whom Dante has borrowed from Cicero.

In the next, or third pit (Canto xix.), we again find fire as the instrument with which the sinners are punished. Those who have made money by misuse of sacred offices are buried head downwards in holes with their feet projecting, and fire plays about their soles. Naturally an opportunity is here presented for some strong invective against the recent unworthy occupants of the See of Rome.

Canto xx. brings us to the fourth pit, in which those who have professed to foretell the future march in a dismal procession with their heads turned round so that they look down their own backs. The sight of Manto, daughter of Tiresias, suggests a description of the origin of the city of Mantua. The last lines of this canto contain one of the most important indications of time which Dante gives in this part of the poem.

The sinners of the fifth pit correspond in some degree with those of the third, except that in their case the traffic which is punished has to do with secular offices. Canto xxi. opens with the famous description of the work in the arsenal of Venice, which is introduced in order to afford an image of the boiling pitch in which sinners of this class are immersed. For some reason, which is not very clear, Dante devotes two whole cantos to this subdivision of the subject. There is no doubt that *baratteria*, peculation or jobbery, was rampant throughout Southern Europe at the time, and, as has been said, it was one of the charges brought against the poet himself at the time of his banishment.* We find here again one of "the torments of heat;" with one exception, that of the evil counsellors in Canto xxv., the last instance in which heat plays a part. It would be interesting, by comparison of the various sins into the punishment of which it enters, to see if any ground can be suggested for its employment in their case.

Cantos xxi. and xxii. are also noteworthy as bringing into prominence the agency of devils, and showing them actually at work. Ten are introduced and named; and some indication is given of their organisation. Dante's skill is perhaps nowhere more apparent than in the way in which he has surmounted the difficulty of depicting beings in whom there is no touch of any good quality. They are plausible; and their leader, Malacoda, appears at first sight almost friendly. It is not until later that his apparent friendliness turns out to be a deliberate attempt to mislead.

* See p. 79.

At the opening of Canto xxiii. we find the poets exactly half-way through Malebolge, on the rocky table-land, so to call it, which separates the fifth and sixth pits. They are quite solitary, for the first time in the course of their journey out of sight and hearing of any other beings; but still in fear of pursuit from the fiends whom they have just left. These do not, however, come up until just as the poets have begun the descent into the sixth pit, and here their power is at an end.

In this pit are punished the hypocrites, who go in slow procession clad in cowls of gilded lead. Contrary to the usual practice the poets have in this case to descend to the bottom of the pit, the bridges being all broken away. Malacoda, the leader of the fiends in the last *bolgia*, had mentioned one, but (falsely) assured them that they would find a sound one further on. He also informed them that the destruction of the bridges had taken place 1266 years ago on the previous day, but five hours later than the time of speaking. This gives an important "time-reference." There can be no doubt that the allusion is to the rending of the rocks at the moment of Our Lord's death (*cf.* xii. 31-45), which took place at 3 P.M., so that we have 10 A.M. on Easter Eve fixed as the hour at which the poets meet with the devils of the fifth pit. Among the hypocrites Dante talks with two men who had jointly held the office of *Podestà*, or chief magistrate, at Florence in the year after his birth.* They belonged to opposite parties, and the double appointment had been one of the many expedients devised to restore peace; but it had not answered, and the two were suspected of having sunk their own differences of opinion, not to conciliate the factions, but to enrich themselves at the expense of the State. While talking to them Dante sees a figure fastened to the ground with three stakes, as though crucified. This, it is explained, is Caiaphas; Annas being similarly placed at another point of the circle. Dante and Virgil have to leave this pit as they entered it, by climbing over the rocks (Canto xxiv.); and from the minuteness with which this process is described (even to so characteristic a touch as "I talked as I went, to show that my wind was good,") it has been thought that Dante was not without experience in mountain-craft.

* See p. 36.

The seventh pit is appointed for the punishment of thieves. Serpents and dragons are here introduced. In some cases the body is reduced to ashes in consequence of the bite, and presently recovers its shape; in others man and serpent blend; in others, again, they exchange natures, the sinners themselves being transmuted into the reptiles, and becoming the instruments of torment to their fellows. A kind of reckless and brutal joviality seems to characterise the malefactors whom we meet with in this region. Among them are many Florentines, a fact which prompts Dante to an apostrophe full of bitter irony, with which Canto xxvi. opens. In the following pit a curious change of tone is manifest. The image chosen to illustrate the scene is an agreeable one—fireflies flitting in summer about a mountain valley; and the punishment though terrible is in no way loathsome or degrading, like most of those which have hitherto been described in the present circle. The sinners, too, who are mentioned are men who on earth had played heroic parts; the manner of their speech is dignified, and Dante treats them with respect. They are those who have sinned by giving wicked counsel to others, and so leading them to commit sin; and the two who are especially distinguished and who relate their stories at length are Ulysses (Canto xxvi.) and Count Guy of Montefeltro, a great Ghibeline leader (xxvii.). The former probably owes his place here to Virgil's epithet *scelerum inventor*, deviser of crimes. In a passage which has deservedly become famous, he gratifies Dante's curiosity as to the manner of his end. The passage, apart from its poetic beauty, is remarkable as being, so far as can be traced, due entirely to the poet's own invention. At all events, beyond two or three words in the *Odyssey*, nothing in either classical or mediæval legend is known which can have given the suggestion for it. In the case of the Count of Montefeltro, who is alleged to have given treacherous counsel to Boniface VIII., it also appears difficult to understand how the facts, if facts they are, became known to Dante. Villani no doubt gives the story, but in language so similar to that of the poem that a suspicion arises whether he may not be relying on it as his authority.

The next canto (xxviii.) introduces us to one of Dante's most ghastly conceptions. The ninth pit is peopled by those who have on earth caused strife and divisions among mankind. They are not, as often stated, schismatics in the technical sense of the word. Mahommed and Ali are there, obviously not on religious grounds however, but as having brought about a great breach between divisions of the human race; and though Fra Dolcino, who is introduced as it were by anticipation, was a religious schismatic, it was no doubt his social heterodoxy which earned him a commemoration in this place. The punishment of these sinners is appropriate. They are constantly being slashed to pieces by demons; the wounds being closed again before they complete the circuit. Curio, who as Lucan narrates, spoke the words which finally decided Cæsar to enter upon civil war, Mosca de' Lamberti, the instigator of the crime which first imported especial bitterness into the strife of factions at Florence, and one Peter of Medicina, who seems to have devoted himself to keeping party-spirit alive in Romagna, are here. Last of all, carrying his own head like a lantern, is Bertrand of Born, the famous troubadour, who is charged with having promoted the quarrel between Henry II. of England and his son. It is worth noting that at this point we get the first definite indication of the dimensions which Dante assumes for the present division of Hell. We are told that this ninth pit of Malebolge has a circumference of twenty-two miles. From the next canto we learn that the last or innermost pit has half this measure; and from this basis it has been found possible to draw an accurate plan of Malebolge, and to conjecture, with an approach to certainty, the conception formed by Dante of Hell generally.*

In the last pit (Cantos xxix. and xxx.) are found those who have been guilty of personation with criminal intent, or of bearing false witness, or of debasing the coinage or pretending to transmute metals. These suffer from leprosy, dropsy, raving madness, and other diseases. Before leaving the pit, a quarrel between two of the sinners attracts Dante's attention more than Virgil thinks seemly; and a sharp reprimand follows. Dante's penitence however earns speedy forgiveness.

We are now drawing near the lowest pit; and through the dim air is heard the sound of a great

---

* It seems never to have been noticed that, as every line from the surface to the centre is perpendicular, a descent by *slopes*, such as is represented, would really be impossible.

horn (Canto xxxi.) Going forward, they find that the final descent, which appears to be a sheer drop of about thirty-five feet, is guarded by a ring of giants. Those of them who are seen are Nimrod, and the classical Ephialtes and Antæus; but we learn that others famous in Greek mythology are there also. Antæus being addressed by Virgil in courteous words, lifts the poets down the wall and lands them on the lowest floor of Hell. This (Canto xxxii.) is of ice, and must be conceived as a circular plain, perhaps about two miles in diameter. In this are punished all who have been guilty of any treachery towards those to whom they were bound by special ties of kindred, fellow-citizenship, friendship, or gratitude. Each of these various grades of crime has its own division, and these are arranged concentrically, with no very definite boundaries between the different classes. At the same time each division has its appropriate name, formed from some famous malefactor who had specially exemplified that class of crime. Thus the first ring is Caina; the second, Antenora, from Antenor, who, according to a late version of the Trojan legend, had betrayed Troy to the Greeks; the third,

Toommea, from that Ptolemy, son of Abubus, who treacherously slew the Maccabees at a feast; the last, in which Lucifer himself abides, is Giudecca. No distinction appears to exist between the penalties inflicted on the two first classes; all are alike plunged up to the shoulders in the ice, the head being free. Dante speaks with more than one, most of them persons who had belonged to the Ghibeline party; though in the case of one, Bocca degli Abati, the treachery had been committed to the detriment of the Guelfs.* The mention of Bocca and Dante's behaviour to him, may remind us that the whole question of Dante's demeanour towards the persons whom he meets in the first part of the poem is interesting. For some he is full of pity, towards some he is even respectful; occasionally he is neutral; while in some cases he displays anger and scorn, amounting as here to positive cruelty, The expressions of pity, it will be observed, practically cease from the moment that Malebolge, the "nethermost Hell," is reached. Similarly, after reaching the City of Dis, the tone of Virgil towards the guardians of the damned, which up to that point

* See p. 34.

has been peremptory, becomes almost suppliant
The reason for this is indeed somewhat obscure:
one does not at once see why the formula "So it is
willed there, where will is power," should not be as
good for the Furies or for Malacoda as it has proved
for Charon and Minos. Perhaps the clue is to be
found in the fact that the sins punished *inside* the
walls of the city (sins which, it will be seen, are not
represented in Purgatory at all) are to be regarded
as the result of a will obstinately set against the
will of God; while the sins arising from the frailty
of human nature may be checked by the "right
judgement" recalling, before it is too late, what the
will of God is. This, however, is a different question, and we must not here pursue it too far. To
revert to that of Dante's various demeanour, it will
be seen that, with the limitation indicated above,
his sympathy with the sinner does not vary with
the comparative heinousness of the sin. Almost
his bitterest scorn, indeed, is directed towards some
whose chief sin is lack of any positive qualities, good
or bad. One infers that he would almost rather
wander in a flame with Ulysses, or lie in the ice
with Ugolino, than undergo the milder punishment

of Celestine and his ignoble companions. For the simply self-indulgent, Francesca or Ciacco, he has pity in abundance; Farinata, Brunetto, and the other famous men who share the fates of these, may probably come into the same category. In such cases as these, while he has not a word to say against the justice of God, he has no desire to add "the wrath of man" thereto. In the one instance in Malebolge where he shows any sympathy (and is reproved by Virgil for doing so) it is for the soothsayers, whose sin would not necessarily involve the hurt of others. But his conduct is very different to those whose sin has been primarily against their fellow-man, or against kindly human intercourse. His first fierce outbreak is against the swaggering ruffian Filippo Argenti, who seems to have been in Florentine society the most notable example of a class now happily extinct in civilised countries, at all events among adults; a kind of bully, or "Mohock," fond of rough practical jokes, prompted, not by a misguided sense of humour, but by an irritable man's delight in venting his spite. One can sympathise, even after six hundred years, in Dante's pious satisfaction when he saw the man, of whom he may himself have once gone in bodily fear, become in his turn the object of persecution. It is, however, after Malebolge is reached, and Dante is among the sinners who have by dishonest practices weakened the bond of confidence which should bind human society together, that he lets his wrath and scorn have full play. His imagery even takes on a grotesque, at times even a foul aspect. He was not one to mince his words, and if he means to sicken his readers, he goes straight to his aim.

It is to be noted, too, that the language and demeanour of the sinners themselves have in many cases changed. Above Malebolge, at all events till the usurers are reached, a certain dignity of speech and action is the rule. Now we find flippant expressions and vulgar gestures. Nothing is omitted which can give a notion, not merely of the sinfulness, but of the sordidness of dishonesty. Curiously enough, the one denizen of this region who is thoroughly dignified and even pathetic, is the pagan Ulysses; and to him Dante does not himself speak, leaving the pagan Virgil to hold all communication with him. Besides Ulysses, Guy of Montfeltro and Ugolino are presented in such a way as to enlist, in some degree, the sympathy of the reader; and it may further be noted that in each case a representative of the family in the next generation is placed in Purgatory; as though Dante, while bound to condemn the elder men, had held the houses in such esteem that he wished to balance the condemnation by assigning a better fate to their successors.

The opening of Canto xxxiii. brings us to the famous episode of Count Ugolino, which shares with the earlier one of Francesca da Rimini the widest renown of any passage in the whole poem. It is curious, by the way, that the structure of the two shows many marked parallelisms; only the tender pity which characterises Dante's treatment of the former is wholly lacking in the latter. There is no need to dwell on so well-known a story; but it may be noted that Ugolino, though a Guelf leader, and condemned here no doubt for his intrigues with the Ghibeline Archbishop Roger, came of a Ghibeline family, and thus forms only a partial exception to the rule stated above. The only genuine Guelf who is named in this division is Tesauro de' Beccheria, the Abbot of Vallombrosa.

This will perhaps be the best point at which to

say a few words on a subject about which much misconception has prevailed. It has often been supposed that Dante was just a Ghibeline partisan, and distributed his characters in the next world according to political sympathies. The truth is, that under no circumstances, so far as we can see, does he assign to any one his place on political grounds—that is, merely for having belonged to one or other of the great parties which then divided Italy. He himself, as we know, belonged to neither. His political ideal was a united world submitting to the general direction of the Emperor in temporal matters, of the Pope in spiritual. On the other hand, he would have had national forms of government retained. Brought up as he had been, the citizen and afterwards the official of a Guelf republic, there is no reason to suppose that a republican form of government was in any way distasteful to him, provided that it was honestly administered. It was not until the more powerful faction in the Guelf party called in the aid of an external power, unconnected with Italy, and hostile, or, as he would doubtless hold, rebellious, to the Empire, that he, along with the more "constitutional" branch of the Guelfs, threw in his lot with the long-banished Ghibelines. But neither then nor at any time did he belong to the Ghibeline party. So far from it, that he takes that party (in *Par.*, vi. 105) as the example of those who follow the imperial standard in the wrong way, and make it a symbol of iniquity. The greatest and most heroic figure in the whole history of the Ghibelines, the man whose love for the rebellious city was as great as Dante's own, who when he had by his prowess in arms recovered it for the Empire, stood resolutely between it and the destruction which in the opinion of his comrades it had merited, is condemned to share with a Pope and an Emperor the penalty of speculative heterodoxy. On the other hand, we find Charles of Anjou, the foreign intruder, the bitter foe of the Empire and pitiless exterminator of the imperial race, a man in whom later historians, free from personal or patriotic bias, have seen hardly any virtue to redeem the sombre cruelty of his career, placed, not indeed in Paradise, but in Purgatory, and waiting in sure and certain hope of ultimate salvation, as one who in spite of many faults had led a pure and ascetic life in a profligate and self-indulgent age. It would be interesting to know, if Dante had met Charles somewhat later, in which of the Purgatorial circles he would have placed him. He seems to evade the difficulty of classifying him by finding him where he does.

It is necessary to insist rather strongly on this point, since even so accomplished a scholar as the late Professor Bartoli, when dealing with Dante's reference to the Emperor Henry VII. (in *Par.*, xxx. 133, sqq.), forgets that all the saints in Paradise have their allotted seat in the Rose of the highest heaven, and speaks as though Dante had honoured Henry above all but the greatest saints and foretold his "direct flight from the earth to the Empyrean." Of course there is not a word of this. All that we are entitled to say is that Dante held Henry to be an Emperor who was doing his duty, and would earn his reward like any other Christian and before Dante himself. It will be observed that he sees no other Emperor in Paradise, save Charlemagne; one, Rudolf of Hapsburg, is in, or rather just outside of, Purgatory; one, the great Frederick II., in Hell. Of the Popes one only, and he a Pope who in his life lay under grievous suspicion of heterodoxy, and moreover only occupied the Papal See for a few months, is placed in Heaven. This is "Peter of Spain," Pope John XXI. Two are in Purgatory; one of them, Martin IV., being a man who, as a Frenchman by birth, and a strong partisan of Charles of Anjou, might be supposed to have been specially obnoxious to Dante. No doubt Popes appear in what may seem an unfair proportion among the guilty souls below; but even for this distribution Dante could probably have pleaded orthodox authority and certainly scriptural support. "To whom much is given, of the same shall much be required." It is true, as Professor Bartoli points out, that Dante's "reverence for the supreme keys" was compatible with a very low estimate of their holders; but is not this exactly what we should expect from a man of high ideals and intolerant of failure in proportion to the dignity of the aim? His treatment of Pope Celestine, the one Pope of his time from whom, *prima facie*, something other than political partisanship might have been hoped, and who having put his hand to the plough had looked back, is sufficient to indicate his attitude in this matter.

Once realise that Dante was, like our own Milton, a man with a keen sense of what ought to be, and an equally keen appreciation of the fact that things in his time were by no means as they ought to be, that he was fallen on evil days and evil tongues—an appreciation which doubtless most great souls, short of the few greatest, have had at most periods of the world's history—and you have the key to much that no ordinary theory of party-spirit will explain. Men of this temper care little for the party cries of everyday politics; and yet they cannot quite sit outside the world of affairs and watch the players, as we may imagine Shakespeare to have done, in calm consciousness that the shaping of our rough-hewn ends was in other hands than ours. No great historian of Shakespeare's time devoted a whole chapter to his memory, as did Villani to that of Dante; yet we can hardly doubt that in the education of the world Shakespeare has borne the more important share, and Dante, with his deep conviction of the higher dignity of the "contemplative life," would be the first to own it.

The third subdivision, known as Tolommea, has,

as one of its inmates says, the "privilege" of receiving the souls of sinners while their bodies are yet alive on earth, animated by demons. With this horrible conception we seem to have reached the highest mark of Dante's inventive power. Only two names are mentioned, but one feels that if the owners of them ever came across the poem in which they had earned so sinister a commemoration, their sentiment towards the poet would hardly be one of gratitude.* These are the last of his contemporaries whom Dante brands, the last, indeed, whom he recognises. In Giudecca (Canto xxxiv.) the sinners are wholly sunk below the ice, and only show through like straws or other small impurities in glass. An exception is made in the case of the three persons whom Dante regards as having carried the sin of ingratitude to its highest point. Lucifer, who, as has been said, is fixed at the lowest point, has three faces. In the mouth of the central one he for ever gnaws Judas Iscariot, while in the others are Brutus and Cassius.

* A late legend, to which some eminent writers have given too easy credence, does actually assert that Dante did go to Genoa, in the suite of Henry VII., about the end of 1311, and there was ill-used by some of Branca d'Oria's friends or domestics. But none of the early commentators knows anything of this tale.

The journey to the upper world is begun by a climb down the shaggy sides of the Archfiend himself. On reaching his middle, which is also the centre of the earth, the position is reversed, and the ascent begins. For a short distance they climb up by Lucifer's legs, then through a chimney in the rock; lastly, it would appear, following the course of a stream which winds spirally down through the earth, they reach the surface, and again come in sight of the stars.

§ 2. Purgatory.

After the invocation to the Muses, a curious survival of classical imagery with which in one form or another each division of the poem begins, Dante relates how, on emerging from the lower world, as Easter Day was dawning the poets found themselves on an island with the first gleam of day just visible on the distant sea. Venus is shining in the eastern heaven; and four stars, "never seen save by the earliest of mankind," are visible to the south. No doubt some tradition or report of the Southern Cross had reached men's ears in Europe; but the symbolical meaning is more important, and there can be no doubt that the stars denote the four "cardinal" or natural or active virtues of fortitude, temperance, justice, and prudence. In the evening, as we shall see later on, their place is taken by three other stars, which symbolise the theological or Christian or contemplative virtues—faith, hope, charity.

On turning again Dante sees close at hand an old man of venerable countenance, who questions them by what right they had come. Virgil recognises him for Cato of Utica, the Roman Republican patriot. His position here, as warder of the mount of purification, is very curious, and has never been thoroughly explained. Among other things it is probable that Dante was influenced by the Virgilian line in which Cato is introduced as the lawgiver of good men in the after-world. Being satisfied with the explanation given, Cato directs them to the shore, where Virgil is to wash the grime of Hell from Dante's face, and gird him with a rush, as an emblem of humility. When this has been done and as the sun is rising (Canto ii.) a light is seen approaching over the water. As it draws near, it is seen to be an angel. His wings form the sails to a boat which comes to the shore, freighted with more than a hundred souls on their way to Purgatory. They are chanting the Easter Psalm *In exitu Israel;* at the sign of the cross made by the angel they come ashore, and begin by inquiring the way of Virgil. While he is explaining that he is no less strange to the country than they are, some of them perceive that Dante is a living man, and all crowd around him. Among them he recognises a friend, the musician Casella, who, after some affectionate words have passed between them, begins at Dante's request to sing one of the poet's own odes; and the crowd listen intently. But Cato comes up, and bidding them delay no longer, drives them like a flock of frightened pigeons towards the mountain.

Even Virgil is somewhat abashed on account of his participation in the delay (Canto iii.); but soon recovers his equanimity, and resumes his usual dignified pace. Dante for the first time observes that his companion casts no shadow on the ground, and Virgil explaining that the spiritual form, while capable of feeling pain, has not the property of intercepting light, takes occasion to point out that there are mysteries for which the human reason is unable to account, and that this very inability forms the chief unhappiness of the great thinkers whom they saw among the virtuous heathen on the border of Hell. With this they reach the foot of the mountain of Purgatory. As is explained elsewhere, this occupies a position exactly opposite to the conical pit of Hell; being indeed formed of that portion of the earth which fled at the approach of Satan when he fell from Heaven. Some of its features are no doubt borrowed from the legendary accounts which Pliny and others have preserved of a great mountain seen by navigators to the west of the Straits of Gibraltar; these accounts being probably based on imperfect descriptions of Atlas or Teneriffe, or both confused together. Its summit is exactly at the Antipodes of Jerusalem, a point which must be carefully borne in mind if the various astronomical indications of time given in the course of the journey are to be rightly understood.

The mountain-side, which Dante compares to the steepest and most rugged parts of the Genoese Riviera, appears at first quite inaccessible; but before long they meet a company of spirits, who, after recovering from their first astonishment at seeing from Dante's shadow that he is not one of themselves, indicate to them the point at which the cliff may be attacked. Before they proceed further, one of the shades addressing Dante makes himself known as Manfred, son to the Emperor Frederick II., and gives an account of his end, explaining that excommunication—for he had died under the ban of the Church—is powerless to do more than protract the interval between the soul's admission to Purgatory. After this (Canto iv.) they enter a steep and narrow cleft in the rock, from which they emerge upon a ledge on the mountain face, and a further climb up this lands them about noon on a broader terrace. Hitherto they have been mounting from the eastward, and on looking back in that direction, Dante is surprised to find the sun on his left hand. Virgil explains the topography; and is saying, in order to encourage Dante, that the labour of climbing will diminish as they get higher, when a bantering voice interrupts with the assurance that he will need plenty of sitting yet. The poet recognises in the speaker a Florentine friend. Another playful sarcasm on his thirst for information makes Dante address the shade and inquire as to his state.

He, like Manfred, is debarred from entering Purgatory, but on the ground that he had led an easy life, and taken no thought of serious matters till his end drew near. In the following cantos (v. and vi.) we meet with many spirits who are from various causes in a similar position. First come those who have been cut off in the midst of their sins, but have sought for mercy at the last. The most noteworthy of these is Buonconte of Montefeltro, son of that Count Guy whom we met in the eighth pit o Malebolge. He was slain fighting against the Florentines at the battle of Campaldino (1289), in which Dante himself may possibly have borne arms.*
Four lines at the end of this canto are among the most famous in the poem. In a few words they commemorate one of the domestic tragedies which were only too familiar in mediæval Italy. Passing through the crowd, they fall in, as evening is drawng on, with a solitary shade, who replies to Virgil's inquiry for the best road by asking whence they come. At the answer, "Mantua," the shade springs up, and reveals himself as the famous warrior-poet of that city, Sordello. The affectionate greeting

* But see p. 42.

which follows between the fellow-citizens moves Dante to a splendid denunciation of the internecine quarrels then raging throughout Italy, and of the neglect on the part of the divinely ordained monarch, the Roman Emperor, which has allowed matters to come to such a pass. Lastly he directs his invective especially against his own city, Florence, and in words of bitter sarcasm upbraids her with the perpetual revolutions which hinder all good government.

Sordello is an example of those whom constant occupation in affairs of state had caused to defer any thought for spiritual things, and who are expiating the delay in the region outside the proper entrance to Purgatory. In Canto vii., after explaining that they will not be able to stir a step after sunset ("the night cometh when no man can work"), he leads the poets to a spot where they may pass the night. This is a flowery dell on the hillside, occupied by the spirits of those who in life had been sovereign princes and rulers. There they see the Emperor Rudolf and his adversary, Ottocar of Bohemia; Charles of Anjou, King of Naples and Sicily, Philip III. of France, Peter III. of Aragon, Henry III. of England, and many other famous men of the last generation. Sordello, in pointing them out, takes occasion to enlarge on the degeneracy of their sons, making a special exception in favour of Edward, son of Henry.

The sun sets (Canto viii.) and the shades join in the Compline hymn. At its conclusion, two angels clad in green robes descend, and take up their position on either side of the little valley. Dante, with his companions, goes down to join the "mighty shades," and is met by one whom he at once recognises as an old friend, the Pisan noble Giovanni, or Nino de' Visconti, "judge" or governor of the Sardinian province called Gallura, nephew of Count Ugolino. After some talk Dante notices the three stars spoken of above, and at the same moment Sordello draws Virgil's attention to an "adversary." They see a serpent making its way through the grass; and immediately the angels start in pursuit, putting it to flight. After this episode another shade announces himself as Conrad Malaspina, of the house with whom Dante was to find shelter during a part of his exile.

The night wears on, and Dante falls asleep (Canto ix.). He dreams that he is being carried by an eagle up to the empyrean heaven. On awaking he finds that the sun has risen some time, and learns from Virgil that at daybreak St. Lucy (who has already come under notice as taking an interest in his welfare) had appeared and borne him to the place where they now are, in front of the gate of Purgatory. This is approached by three steps of variously-coloured stone. The first is white marble, the second a dark and rough rock, the third blood-red porphyry, indicating probably the three stages of the soul's progress to freedom through confession, contrition, and penance. On the topmost step sits an angel, who having marked seven P's (*peccata* sins) on Dante's forehead, admits them within the gate.

Thus far, except in the passage, Canto viii. 19 sqq., to which Dante himself draws the reader's attention, the allegorical interpretation has not afforded any very great difficulty. With this particular passage readers will do well to compare *Inf.*, ix. 37 sqq., where a very similar indication is given of an underlying allegory, and draw their own conclusions. But on the whole, the main interest of the first nine cantos of the *Purgatory* is more of a personal nature.

Sordello alone may give an excuse for a good deal of historical research. For example, no one has yet explained Dante's reasons for so distinguishing a person who, from all the records that we have, does not seem to have made any great figure in the eyes of his contemporaries.

It will hardly be necessary to follow Dante step by step through the stages of the mountain of purification. We shall probably do best to consider the general plan on which Purgatory is arranged, the nature of the various penances, with their adaptation to the offences which they expiate, and the light thrown in this division of the poem on Dante's opinions about the elements of political and moral science.

We find, then, seven cornices, or ledges, on the mountain, connected with each other by stairways cut in the rock. Each stairway is guarded by an angel, and each, as it would appear, is shorter and less steep than the previous one. Thus the passage from the first to the second circle takes a considerable time, enough at all events to allow of some conversation between Dante and Virgil between the moment of their passing the angel and that at which they reach the top of the stairway. On the other hand, when they come to the final ascent, from the seventh circle to the level of the Earthly Paradise which occupies the summit, a few steps are sufficient to bring them to their halting-place, which, as appears afterwards, is practically on the summit level. Each angel, as Dante passes, erases from his forehead one of the P's which the warder of the first gate had inscribed there, and utters one of the Scriptural Beatitudes appropriate to the circle which they are quitting. Thus, "Blessed are the peacemakers" accompanies their departure from the circle of the wrathful; "Blessed are they that hunger after righteousness" is heard as they leave that where gluttony is expiated.

The ritual, so to speak, is very precise throughout. Besides the Beatitudes, which are recited by the angel-guards, and in some cases it would seem repeated by a chorus of voices, we find in each circle commemoration variously contrived of notable instances, both of the sins punished and of their "contrary virtues." These are perhaps worth going through in detail. In the circle of

Pride, where it is necessary to go in a stooping posture, the pavement is engraved with representations of humility. The first is the Annunciation, (and here it should be noted that in every group an event from the life of the Virgin holds the first place); next comes David dancing before the Ark; and lastly, Trajan yielding to the widow's prayer that he would perform an act of justice before setting out with the pomp of a military expedition. Further on in the same circle are found examples of the punishment of pride, taken alternately from Scripture and from classical mythology. The next circle is that of Envy. Here the penalty consists of the sewing up of the eyes, so that pictured representations would be of no use; and, accordingly, the task of calling the examples to mind is discharged by voices flying through the air. Yet another method is adopted in the third circle, where the Angry are punished by means of a dense smoke. Here the pictures are conveyed to Dante's mind by a kind of trance or vision, in which he sees the various scenes. We must suppose that the spirits pass through some similar experience. In the fourth circle, the examples of activity and warnings against Sloth are delivered by the souls themselves. As it is night while Dante is in this circle, he is himself unable to move; but the discipline being to run at speed, the souls pass him in their course. The fifth circle, of the Avaricious and Prodigal, follows much the same rule as the fourth, except that here the instances of virtue are recited in the day, those of sin at night, so that Dante does not actually hear the latter. In this case the souls lie prostrate. The Gluttonous, in the sixth circle, are punished by having to pass under trees laden with fruit, which they cannot reach; and the examples and warnings are conveyed by voices among the branches of these trees. The seventh circle follows the fashion of the fourth, except that the souls (who are punished by fire for having in life failed to hold in due restraint the flames of passion) seem to address the warning reminiscences to each other as they meet in the circuit. An instance of the system on which the examples are introduced has been given from the first circle. Perhaps that for the sixth is even more typical. On first entering this they come to a tree, among the branches of which a voice is heard recording the conduct of the Virgin at the feast in Cana, when "she thought more of the success of the banquet than of her own mouth;" the custom of drinking only water prevalent among the Roman women, and the abstemiousness of Daniel and the Baptist. Then, after passing through a portion of the circle, and holding converse with its inmates, they reach another tree, from which a second voice comes to them bidding them remember the trouble that came from the drunkenness of the Centaur at the wedding of Pirithous, and the rejection by Gideon of the men who had drunk immoderately. This coupling of a classical and Scriptural instance is quite invariable.

To pass on to the subject of the light thrown upon Dante's speculative views in the *Purgatory*. It is not too much to say that from that point of view it is the most important division of the whole poem. This, perhaps, follows naturally from its subject. The Purgatorial existence bears more affinity to the life of this world than does that of those who have reached their eternal abode; and human affections and human interests still have much of their old power. This, then, would naturally be the division in which questions arising from the conditions of man's life with men would be likely to suggest themselves.

In the *Hell* we had indeed a statement of Dante's view of Ethics, so far as was necessary to explain his attitude towards breaches of the moral law and their punishment. In the *Purgatory* he goes more deeply into the question, and expounds in Cantos xvi., xvii., and xviii., a theory with regard to the origin of morals and knowledge. According to this the soul when created is a *tabula rasa*, but having certain capacities inherent in it in consequence of the nature of its Creator. The Creator being absolutely veracious, the information imparted by the senses is infallible. Further, the Creator being absolutely happy, the soul naturally seeks happiness, and is said to love that in which it expects to find happiness. So far there is no room for error. Where it can come in is in the inferences which the mind draws from the information which the senses give, and in either its choice of an object to love, or the vigour with which it pursues that object. It must be further noted that the soul is endowed at the outset with a knowledge of good and evil, *i.e.* conscience, and with free-will; though this latter has to struggle with the conditions which the influence of the heavenly bodies imposes on the individual. With due culture, however, it can ultimately prevail over these; but it must also be aided in its struggle by the check of law and the guidance which should be afforded by spiritual pastors. In order that these may have their full effect, it is desirable that the secular and spiritual authorities should be in different hands: and thus we are brought to the same conclusions as in the treatise *De Monarchia*.

To return, however, to the moral question. All action, as has been said, is directed to an end, and (in the words of Aquinas, following Aristotle) the end for each individual is that which he desires and loves. If the end is rightly selected, and the love duly proportioned, the action does not incur blame. But it may happen that the end may be evil; in which case evil becomes the object of the love, or the love is turned to hatred. Now, no created being can hate its Creator, nor can any man hate himself; therefore the sins arising from this cause must be sins against fellow-men. These, so far as Purgatory is concerned, are pride, envy, anger, which, when carried into action, become the sins that are punished within the City of Dis, though in Purgatory they would appear on the whole to be regarded as the less grave offences.

When the object is good, but the love is lacking in due vigour, we have the sin of sloth, or, as our forefathers called it, "accidie." This occupies a somewhat anomalous position. Those who have allowed it to grow to moodiness and given way to it past hope of repentance, lie in Hell at the bottom of the Stygian marsh, and nothing is seen of them but the bubbles which are formed by their sighs; while the wrathful or ill-tempered lie in the same marsh, but appear above the water. Both sins alike render the man full of hatred for his fellows, and make him insensible to the joy of life. In Purgatory, on the other hand, the anger which is punished seems rather to be the fault of hasty temper; while in the case of sloth, the souls who expiate it are represented as running at great speed, and proclaiming instances of conspicuous alertness. For our present purpose, then, it must be regarded as merely slothfulness or indolence.

Finally, we have the cases in which the object is natural, or even laudable. A fair share of this world's goods, our daily food, the love between man and woman, all these are objects to which the desires may lawfully be directed, so long as they are duly restrained. When, however, they become the main aim, they are sinful, and lead to the sins for which the discipline of the three upper cornices is required; the most severe of all that is undergone in Purgatory. Yet these are the sins which in Hell "incur less blame," as being sins involving rather the animal than the spiritual part of man. But there is not space here to discuss this aspect of the subject. Readers will find much interest in working it out for themselves.

The physiological sketch given by Statius in the twenty-fifth canto, introduced to account for the spiritual body, is in logical order an introduction to Dante's ethics and psychology; and is remarkable both in its agreement with Aristotle and its divergence from him. The occasion for it is found in a question raised by Dante, and suggested to him by the appearance of the shades in the circle which they have just left: namely, how beings who have no need to go through the ordinary process of nutrition, can feel the desire for food (as Forese has explained that they do) and grow lean through the deprivation of it. In order to solve this difficulty, Statius sketches briefly the stages of the development of the human being, from his first conception until he has an independent existence, showing how the embryo progresses first to vegetative then to animal life, and how finally, when the brain is complete (this being the last stage in the organisation), the "First Mover" breathes the human soul into the frame. The soul, having thus an independent existence, when the frame decays sets itself loose therefrom, taking with it the senses and passions, as well as the mental faculties of memory, understanding, and will. The latter are still in full activity, but the former have only a potential existence until such time as the soul has found its place in the other world. Then it takes to itself a bodily shape, formed out of the surrounding air (as a flame is formed by the fire), and equips it with organs of sense; and thenceforward this shape is adapted to express all the natural emotions and desires, including of course those of hunger and thirst. This remarkable exposition is based on Aristotle's theory of the generation of the body, and the introduction into it of the soul; but there is an important difference. The Greek philosopher, though his language is not very explicit, has apparently no idea of any survival of the personal identity after death. At all events, so he was interpreted by Averroes and later by Aquinas. With him the source of all movement is the father, from whom only (though here again Aristotle is not quite clear) comes the gift of a soul. Dante, on the contrary, refers these back to the Prime Mover, namely God, and conceives a special creative act as performed on behalf of every human being that is brought into the world. As will be easily seen, this conception is the necessary complement to Dante's system of ethics, based on individual free-will, and postulating a newly-created soul, fresh from the Maker's hand; a *tabula rasa*, with no attributes save the natural propension towards that which gives it pleasure.

We may now pass to the six cantos which

conclude this division of the poem, and form a most important stage in the development of the whole plan. Dante has now proceeded as far as human reason, typified by Virgil, is able to guide him. He is on the threshold of Heaven; but before he can be admitted among the blessed, another conductor must be provided, to whom the way to the Divine Presence shall be freely open. This, of course, can only be knowledge informed by faith, or, as we may say for shortness, theology, not in the sense of a formal science, but in one approaching more nearly to what Aristotle calls *Theoria*, or contemplation. From certain expressions in the earliest cantos of the poem, it is clear that Dante looked upon the woman whom in his youth he had loved, and who had, at the supposed date of these events, been ten years dead, as symbolising this *Theoria*, and as being in some special way entrusted with the task of saving him from spiritual ruin. She accordingly appears, and takes up the duties which Virgil is surrendering. The manner of her appearance must be noticed—showing as it does the almost inextricable web in which Dante combines fact and allegory. That the "Beatrice" who is introduced is primarily none other than an actual woman of flesh and blood, whom hundreds of then living people had known, who had gone about Florence for twenty-four years and married a prominent citizen, and whom Dante had loved with the romantic passion of the Middle Ages, only the misplaced ingenuity of paradoxical critics can doubt.* Yet at her entry she is escorted by a procession, the members of which represent the books of the Bible, the seven virtues, and the gifts of the Holy Spirit; while the car on which she is borne (which itself denotes the Church) is drawn by a mystical figure, in which we cannot fail to see a symbol of the second Person of the Trinity. If it be objected that the salvation of Dante is a small matter about which to set in motion so stupendous a machinery, we may answer that, in the first place, his own salvation does not seem unimportant to the man himself; and further, which is of more weight, that Dante himself is here no less symbolical than Beatrice, or Virgil, or the mystic Gryphon. He is the typical human soul; his experiences, his struggles, his efforts to shake himself free of the trammels of the world and the flesh, are familiar

* See pp. 48-51.

features in the spiritual history of the great majority of Christians. Thus the wonderful pageant described in this canto must be regarded as being displayed, not to him only, but to all Christendom in his person.

A few words with regard to this pageant may afford a little help to its comprehension. After the arrival of Beatrice, a scene follows in which she upbraids Dante for his forgetfulness of her, and receives an avowal of his fault. He is then bathed in the stream of Lethe—another curious employment of pagan mythology—and brought back to the presence of Beatrice. Hitherto she has been veiled; but now, at the special entreaty of her attendant nymphs (those nymphs who are also the four stars in heaven, and denote the cardinal virtues), she withdraws the veil, and discloses again the smile for which her "faithful one" had yearned during ten years.

Soon, however, his attention is called away to new and strange sights. The procession, of which Dante and his remaining companion Statius now form part, moves forward through the wood of the Earthly Paradise; the car is attached to a tree, identified with the "tree of knowledge," which since Adam's disobedience has been leafless and fruitless. After this Dante falls into a short sleep, and on waking finds that Beatrice with her attendants is alone left, as a guardian to the car. Then follow a series of strange transformations, the general plan of which is clearly suggested by the Apocalypse; but their interpretation is to be sought in the relations of the Church to the Empire, down to the time of the "Babylonish captivity," or transference of the Papal See to Avignon. This is symbolised by the departure of the car, drawn this time by a giant (Philip the Fair of France), and occupied no longer by Beatrice, but by a harlot, to denote (again with allusion to the Apocalypse) the corrupt rule under which the Church had fallen.

In the final scene of all, Beatrice, in phrases hardly less obscure than the vision itself, indicates to Dante the lesson which he is to learn from it, and repeats in another form Virgil's prediction of a champion who is to come and set the world to rights. Much has been written about the first of these, the *Veltro;* hardly less about the "five hundred, ten, and five," or DXV. The usual inter-

The "Commedia" 147

pretation takes these letters as intended merely to suggest *Dux*, a leader; but this seems a little weak. Elsewhere I have given reasons for thinking that Dante had a special motive for wrapping up his meaning in this numerical form.

Lastly, in a passage which, though ostensibly only one of Dante's usual time-indications, seems intended to suggest repose after the labours through which he has brought his readers, and the agitation of the last canto, he tells us that at noon they reached the edge of the forest. Here he is made to drink of another stream, Eunoe, or "right mind," after which he is ready for the upward journey.

It is too much to expect readers to work through the voluminous interpretations which have been offered of the very difficult and perplexing mysticism of these cantos. Some points are perhaps plainer to the student who considers them with a fair knowledge of the Bible and history, than to the commentator who wishes to establish a new and original theory. But they are so important (particularly Cantos xxx. and xxxi.) to any one who wishes to understand Dante's whole position as man, poet, scholar, and politician, that they should not be passed over as mere futile mediæval fancies. It should be said, too, that they contain some passages which will never be out of date until the poetic taste of mankind has altogether changed.

§ 3. Paradise.

The first point which will strike the reader on entering upon the third division of the poem is the sudden change in the conditions under which the action is carried on. Hitherto Dante has been moving on solid earth, subject to the usual limitations which are enforced by physical laws upon all human action. Henceforth, as he tells us (*Par.*, xxx. 123), God operates directly, and physical laws have no longer any place. "It is Beatrice," he elsewhere says, "who leads on so swiftly from one stage of blessedness to a higher;" and we shall notice that the transference from sphere to sphere is effected by Dante's fixing his eyes on hers, while she gazes upwards.

A word as to the various spheres may not be out of place here. According to the Ptolemaic system of astronomy, as adapted to the requirements of mediæval belief, the earth was at the centre, and concentric with it were ten hollow spheres. In the first eight of these were placed consecutively the Moon, Mercury, Venus, the Sun, Mars, Jupiter Saturn, and the fixed stars. In order to explain the irregular movements of the planets, "epicycles" or smaller spheres borne by the principal spheres, and bearing the planets, were devised, but these need not be considered here. Outside of the fixed stars came the *primum mobile*, which gave the diurnal revolution of the heavens, and beyond this the Empyrean, or fixed heaven, in which was the special abode of God, and in which all the blessed had their places. Between the earth and the innermost sphere, that of the Moon, lie the regions of water, air, and fire. The Mountain of Purgatory, on the summit of which Dante at the conclusion of the second *Cantica* was standing, lifts its head as far as the third of these. Through this accordingly, Beatrice and Dante have to rise in order to reach the first step in the celestial ascent. It must be noted that there is no reason to suppose that in every case the actual planet is visited. The "heaven" of the planet embraces the whole "sphere" in which it is set, and its characteristics may be conceived as extending to the whole of that sphere.

The fact of rising without apparent motive force through a medium lighter than his own body, at once forms a subject for enquiry on Dante's part; and Beatrice, as she has frequently to do in the course of their journey, resolves his doubt. Those who are reading the poem for the first time will probably pass lightly over these difficult metaphysical passages. They must be read sooner or later by any one who wishes thoroughly to understand Dante's place in the history of speculative thought; but in the first instance it will probably be better to "take them as read" and endeavour to get a clear notion of the general arrangement. There are obvious reasons why this portion of the poem should consist as largely as it does of these subtle disquisitions. There is far less room, in the first place, for variety of description. In a region where there are no shadows, it is impossible to give a detailed picture; and terms indicative of simple brightness are limited. Nor, again, is it easy where all are perfect to depict individual character. Consequently two great elements of interest in the first two parts of the poem are far less available here; and their place must be filled by other matter,

What this matter should be is suggested by the natural division of speculative science into Ethics, or the study of man's conduct as a moral being; Politics, or the science relating to his behaviour in regard to the social order; and Metaphysics, which for Dante is synonymous with theology, the investigation of all that concerns his spiritual part, as well as the Divine order generally. With the first two we have dealt in the *Hell* and the *Purgatory* respectively; the third is reserved for the *Paradise*. Once or twice indeed Dante touches on matters that would seem more fitly to belong to the others; as, for instance, the magnificent passage in Canto vi., where Justinian, after sketching the triumphant course of the Roman Eagle, inveighs against the party feuds of the time; or Carlo Martello's reference to the Sicilian Vespers, and the misdeeds of his brother Robert. But of these the first leads up to an elaborate exposition of the scheme of Redemption, the second seems intended directly to introduce a dissertation on matters lying at the very root of human nature.

To the same difficulty in varying the methods (to use a phrase of Ginguéné's) must be attributed the

occurrence of a good many conceptions which to
our taste appear somewhat grotesque. Yet the better
we know the poem the more we shall feel that
in this third part the author's genius rises to its
sublimest efforts, and agree with the late Dean of
St. Paul's, that it is the true *pierre de touche* of the
student of Dante.

To go briefly through the various stages. The
heaven of the Moon is that in which appear the
spirits of those who having taken vows have under
compulsion or persuasion abandoned them; Mercury contains statesmen and men of affairs; Venus
those who have been over-much swayed by indul
gence in earthly love. It must be observed that,
according to the astronomy of the time, the shadow
of the Earth, cast into space by the Sun, extended
as far as the orbit of Venus. The spirits in these
three spheres therefore form a group by themselves:
being distinguished by the fact that they had allowed
earthly cares and pleasures to obtain too strong
hold of them, to the injury of their spiritual
development. In these three spheres respectively
the representative speakers are Piccarda Donati,
sister of Dante's friend Forese, and of Corso, the

leader of the "Black Guelfs;" the Emperor Justinian; and Carlo Martello, the titular king of Hungary, son of Charles II., king of Naples, who is followed by Cunizza, sister of the Ghibeline chief, Ezzelino da Romano, and Folco of Marseilles, who began as a troubadour and became bishop of his native city.

Although in one sense the inhabitants of the three lower spheres may be said to have attained a less perfect blessedness than those to whom the rest of heaven is assigned, it must not be supposed that they are conscious of any lack. All have their places in the highest or Empyrean heaven, and all sense of sorrow for past imperfections is at an end. We must indeed suppose that, as with Dante himself, the imperfections have been effaced by the discipline of Purgatory, and their remembrance washed away by the water of Lethe.

With the sphere of the Sun, however, we arrive for the first time in the presence of those who have lived so as to earn the full honour of sanctity, and find ourselves amongst canonised saints. Even here Dante has shown himself, as usual, independent of conventional or official restrictions. In his introduction of St. Thomas Aquinas and St. Bonaventura he merely anticipates the formal decision of the Church; but in "Peter of Spain," that is Pope John XXI. (the only historical Pope whom he places in Paradise), he selects for special honour a man who was by no means free from grave suspicion of heresy, and who has never been canonised. As Dante never did anything without a reason we must suppose that some now forgotten merit earned for the Spanish logician a place beside Nathan, Chrysostom, and Anselm. It is by these and such men as these, great teachers and thinkers, that the heaven of the Sun is occupied; the reason no doubt being that as the Sun is the source of light and the promoter of growth in the physical world, so are these in the spiritual.

The tenth canto is specially notable as bringing Dante into the presence of the greatest exponent of the Scholastic philosophy, and the master whom he followed more closely than any other, St. Thomas Aquinas. In the eleventh, the illustrious Dominican recounts the life of St. Francis of Assisi, the founder of the rival order. This is one of the most notable passages in the whole poem, rising as it does to a sustained magnificence of diction which especially characterises those portions of the *Paradise* where the poet allows full play to his genius. Justinian's roll-call of the Roman achievements in Canto vi. is another. Nothing at all like them is found in the two former divisions of the poem; and it is to them that students who wish to feel the attraction which the *Paradise* undoubtedly exercises over those who know it well, should first turn.

The sphere of the Sun, in which we now are, is, it should be noted, one of the two regions of Heaven in which Dante makes the longest stay, the other being that of the Fixed Stars. The passage to it marks a distinct stage in his progress. Looking back to the end of Canto ix. we see that it forms a kind of peroration; while the first twenty-seven lines of Canto x. are, as it were, the introduction to a fresh division of the poem, and recall certain phrases which occurred in the opening canto. It is difficult to say why these two spheres should be made of so much more importance than the rest. Mars is the only one which approaches them; but this is selected by Dante as the scene of his interview with his ancestor Cacciaguida, which gives the occasion for the magnificent contrast between the old days of Florence and its present state, and the prophecy of his own exile; subjects which might well occupy a considerable space. On the other hand, the eulogy of St. Francis, already referred to, which St. Thomas Aquinas delivers, and that of St. Dominic, with which St. Bonaventura, "vying with the courtesy of so mighty a paladin," responds to it, fine as they are, do not appear indispensable in the scheme of the poem. But the whole plan of the *Paradise* is, so far as can be seen, arranged with much less of obvious symmetry than is to be found in the two former *Cantiche*. No doubt the plan is there; but just as "time-indications" for the most part fail us, or can be extracted only by elaborate and somewhat uncertain calculations, so it would seem as if the poet, no longer hampered by the necessities of time and space, had wished to show how he could work with no self-made restrictions.

After his discourse in praise of the founder of the rival order, immediately followed by its counterpart—an eloquent summary of the career of St. Dominic, put into the mouth of the Franciscan Bonaventura — St. Thomas speaks again (Canto xiii.), in order to explain an apparent overestimate of Solomon's greatness among mankind which an expression used by him in naming the spirits present with him might have seemed to imply. As happens more than once in this division of the poem, a piece of what at first sight looks rather like logical quibbling is made the introduction to some profound teaching in reference to the workings of the human mind—teaching which is at least as needful in the present day as it ever was in Dante's own time. Solomon himself then speaks, answering a question put by Beatrice on Dante's behalf as to the nature of the glorified body; and then Dante, having looked upon the countenance of Beatrice, and being by this means (as in every other case) raised "to a higher salvation," finds by the ruddy light which surrounds him that he has entered the sphere of Mars.

A new feature appears here. In each of the three planets exterior (according to the astronomy of that age) to the Sun, we find some special image displayed. In the case of Mars, it is a vast crucifix, composed of spirits, who are darting in all directions within the figure, like motes in a sunbeam. One of them glides from the arm to the foot of the cross, and makes himself known to Dante as his great-great-grandfather, Cacciaguida, probably (though this is not certain) of the family of the Elisei.* He had been, like all the other spirits, as it would seem, of this sphere, a soldier, and had died in battle as a Crusader. The latter half of this, the fifteenth canto, together with the two following, form what is probably the best-known and most frequently quoted portion of the *Paradise*. First we have a beautiful picture of the simple and kindly life of old Florence, before party-spirit and luxury had entered and corrupted its citizens. The picture is, of course, one of those which people in every age have drawn of earlier times, supposed to have been free from the corruptions which each man's experience teaches him are rife in his own day; but none the less it is of value as showing Dante's ideal of social life.

The next canto continues to deal with the same topic; but enters more into detail with regard to

* See p. 38.

the various families, and the vicissitudes in their fortunes. This leads up to the existing strife of parties, and this again naturally to Dante's own share in it, and his exile. It must be remembered that this did not actually come about till two years after the date at which the action of the *Commedia* is supposed to take place; so that the whole is cast into a prophetic form. The language used, however, must be taken as expressing the feeling with which Dante looked back after an interval of nearly twenty years — for the *Paradise* was probably completed very shortly before the poet's death—upon the events in which he had borne a somewhat prominent part. Whether he was ever a personage of the first importance in Florence we may be allowed to doubt. No doubt he was a man of some consideration; but still the office of Prior was one which nearly every eligible citizen must have held;[*] and Villani, who devotes a chapter to his memory, does not mention his name among the political leaders of an earlier period. Probably he occupied among the exiles of 1302 a far less important place in their own eyes and those of

[*] See p. 70.

contemporaries than he does in ours; but if not a leader, he was in the front rank, and must have been aware of all that went on. The passages relating to his exile, to the worthlessness of his companions, to his gratitude towards those who helped him, gain immensely in force and pathos if we regard them as an aging man's reminiscences of a long by-gone time.

With the passage to the sphere of Jupiter (Canto xviii.) the imagery becomes yet more daring. This is the region specially devoted to the spirits of the righteous; and these as they fly are forming letters, which ultimately spell out the opening words of the Book of Wisdom: "Diligite justitiam qui judicatis terram." When the final M is reached a further transformation takes place; the letter is gradually modified into the shape of the imperial eagle. Righteousness, or justice, is, it should be remembered, in Dante's view (as indeed in that of most moralists) the source and foundation of all that goes to establish human society on a virtuous and duly ordered basis. Thus it is rightly illustrated by the symbol of the Empire. The Eagle behaves as one single individual, though composed of countless spirits; speaking with a single voice, and in the singular number. A discourse on justice leads up to a sharp rebuke of nearly every prince then ruling, on the score of misgovernment in one or another form.

After this the Eagle proceeds to indicate whose are the spirits which compose its eye. These with one exception are all great sovereigns of ancient and recent times. The exception is remarkable. In Hell we found several cases in which mythological or fictitious personages were treated on a footing of absolute equality with those who had a perfect historical claim to the distinction; but the appearance in the Christian Heaven of a man whose very name is preserved merely in a single line of the *Æneid* strikes us with astonishment. For being recorded by Virgil as the most righteous man among the Trojans, Rhipeus takes his place beside David, Hezekiah, Constantine, and the "good king" William II. of Sicily.

When the time comes for the ascent to be resumed, Dante notices that Beatrice smiles no longer. On the threshold, as she explains, of the seventh heaven, the lustre of her smile would be more than his eyes could endure. Here, in Saturn, a ladder is seen, reaching to the next sphere. We learn that this is identical with the ladder seen by Jacob in his vision; and down it are descending the spirits of such as in this world had lived the contemplative life in full perfection. The chanting which has been audible in the other spheres is here silent — no doubt in order to symbolise the insensibility to outward impressions of the soul rapt in contemplation. The speakers in this group are St. Peter Damian and St. Benedict; both of whom have severe words to say as to the corruption of the monastic orders.

The company of saints reascend (Canto xxii.): and Dante and Beatrice follow them, mounting by the ladder, but, as it would appear, with no perceptible lapse of time. The eighth heaven, that of the Fixed Stars, is reached in the sign of the Twins; under which Dante himself had been born. At this point Beatrice directs him, before entering on the final blessedness of heaven, and doubtless with the ulterior view of leading him to a just sense of the insignificance of earthly things, to look back over the course which he has traversed.

A very distinct stage of the journey is here reached, and, as has been already noticed, we are entering that one of the celestial spheres in which Dante makes the longest stay.

He and his guide have now reached the outermost of the heavenly spheres of whose existence our senses give any evidence—that of the Fixed Stars. A vision of Christ descending, accompanied by His Mother, and surrounded with saints, is granted to Dante; after which he is again able to endure the effulgence of Beatrice's smile. It is not, however, until Christ has reascended that he recovers his full power of sight. Then he perceives that the company of saints has remained; and presently, at the request of Beatrice, St. Peter comes forward, and proceeds to examine Dante on the subject of Faith, and the grounds for his belief in the Christian revelation. The ensuing colloquy is interesting, as being practically a versified form of the scholastic method of discussion, such as we find in Aquinas. St. Peter plays the part of the supposed opponent, and brings forward the standard objections to Dante's statements of dogma. For the ordinary reader, however, this and the next two cantos form, it must be admitted, one of the less attractive portions of the poem. Yet even here we now and then come upon a passage of pure poetry, such as the famous lines at the opening of Canto xxv., in which Dante utters what must have been almost his last aspiration after a return to "the fair fold in which as a lamb I slept."

Following St. Peter, St. James makes his appearance. To him is entrusted the task of testing Dante's soundness in the doctrine and definition of Hope. Lastly, comes St. John, who examines him touching the right object of Love. In each case, when he has answered to the satisfaction of his questioner, a chant goes up from the assembled spirits; the words on every occasion being taken, as it would appear, from the *Te Deum*. Afterwards the three Apostles are joined by Adam, who takes up the discourse, and answers two unexpressed questions of Dante's, as to the length of his stay in Paradise, and the nature of the primitive language of mankind.

Canto xxvii. opens with a tremendous invective, put into the mouth of St. Peter, against the corruption of the Papacy; a passage which incidentally contains an important piece of evidence with regard to the date at which the later cantos of the *Paradise* were written. A bitter allusion to "men of Cahors" can have been evoked only by the election of John XXII., who was from that city; and he became Pope in 1316. After this the whole multitude of Saints ascend to the highest heaven; but before Dante follows, Beatrice makes him look down once more, and he perceives that since his entry into this sphere he has moved with the diurnal rotation through an arc of forty-five degrees. Then they ascend into the sphere of the First Motion, where place and time no longer exist. From its movement time is measured; and its place is in the Divine intelligence only. Here the Empyrean, or highest Heaven, comes into view; at first as a point of intense brilliancy round which nine circles are revolving. These represent the Angelic hierarchies, and their places with regard to the central point are in inverse order to that of the spheres which they move. Beatrice takes occasion from them to instruct Dante upon some points relating to the creation and functions of the angels, and incidentally, upon the creation of form and matter, and their combination in the visible universe. The passage

(Canto xxix.) is difficult; but is so magnificent in its diction as to deserve careful study. Dante has nowhere else succeeded so completely in clothing with poetry the dry bones of scholastic theology. The discussion, by dealing with several disputed points, gives occasion for some stringent remarks on the preachers of the time.

They now rise to the highest heaven, outside of all the spheres, in which all the blessed have their true place. At first Dante is aware of light only, but gradually a fresh power of sight comes to him, and he sees a river, from and to which bright sparks are ever issuing and returning. The banks are brilliant with flowers. At the command of Beatrice he bows down and drinks, and at once sees the river as a lake of light, the flowers on the banks as concentric rows of saints seated on thrones, and the flitting sparks as angels. At this point Beatrice leaves Dante, after a few scathing words in reference to the "covetousness"* of the Papacy, which has put the world out of joint—words which may be taken

---

* Note that *capidigia* is, in Dante's scheme, the vice opposed to *giustizia*, that which debases nations as righteousness exalts them.

as summing up in brief all the passages throughout the poem in which political affairs are touched upon. With this, if we except one bitter jibe at Florence (xxxi. 39) all controversial matters are dismissed, and the last three cantos of the poem are devoted to a description, rising ever in sublimity, of the joys and mysteries of Heaven.

The "soldiery of heaven" appears in the form of a vast white rose, whose petals are the seats on which the saints sit. On one hand these are filled, being occupied by holy men and women belonging to the old dispensation: while on the other the number of the elect has still to be accomplished. Beatrice having gone back to her place among the blessed beside Rachel, the task of escorting Dante is entrusted to St. Bernard, who points out where some of the more eminent have their stations. As throughout the poem, all is arranged with order and symmetry. The junction between the Old and New Testaments is indicated by the position assigned to Our Lady on one side of the circle, and in the highest row, and St. John the Baptist, who is diametrically opposite to her. Below her sit in order a series of Christ's ancestresses Eve, Rachel,

Sarah, Rebekah, Ruth; Adam is on her left, St. Peter on her right, beyond them Moses and St. John the Evangelist. On either hand of the Baptist sit St. Anne and St. Lucy, and below him a line of founders of orders and other teachers; the lower circles are filled with the spirits of children.

At the close of his enumeration of these chief personages, St. Bernard observes that the time of Dante's slumber is nearly at an end, and that they must, "like a good tailor, cut the coat according to the cloth." In these three lines are two very noticeable points. First, the word "slumber," implying that the whole journey through the other world has been performed in a dream; and secondly, the bold use, at perhaps the most exalted moment of the whole poem, of a trivial, almost vulgar, figure of speech. We meet with other instances of this in the *Paradise*, and they are eminently characteristic of the mediæval mind. The subject is too wide to be discussed here; but readers may be reminded of the numerous examples which the architecture of the period shows, in which grotesque or even indecent figures are introduced among the ornamental work of sacred buildings.

At the beginning of the last canto, St. Bernard, in an address of exquisite beauty (of which Chaucer, in the Second Nun's Tale has given an almost equally exquisite rendering), appeals to the Virgin —who, it will be remembered, is throughout represented as taking a special interest in Dante—for her aid to him in his last and crowning experience. Thus succoured, he is able to gaze upon the Supreme Light; and in a flash there is revealed to him a full comprehension of all fundamental truths, first those of metaphysics, then those of faith. He understands for a moment the whole composition of the universe, and then the mysteries of the Incarnation and the Trinity. The intuition is momentary, and leaves merely the memory of a memory. But the lasting effect is the entire union of his will with the Divine will, and herein, we must understand him to imply, is found the salvation the attainment of which has been the ultimate aim and object of his whole journey.

Many touches in this concluding passage bear a strong resemblance to what seems to have been the teaching of the contemporary German mystics. It would be interesting to inquire how far Dante can have been acquainted with any of the writings of that school. If any connection can be traced, it may throw light on several obscure points.*

It remains to be added that the *Commedia* was first printed at Foligno in 1472. Editions followed in quick succession from Jesi, Mantua, and Naples. The first Venetian edition is that of Vindelin of Spires, in 1477; the first Florentine, that with Landino's commentary, in 1481. It was printed several times more before 1500, and constantly in the sixteenth century. We have several commentaries dating from a period only later by a few years than Dante's death.

* See also p. 16.

CHAPTER VII.

THE MINOR WORKS

THE *Commedia* is, for many readers perhaps, the only book distinctly identified with Dante's name. Yet it must be remembered that, as a matter of fact, it represents less than half of the total bulk of his writings; and, further, that the remainder comprises several works which, though not attaining to the pre-eminent position which all the world now recognises the great poem as occupying, are very remarkable monuments of mediæval literature.

Of the youthful work, the *Vita Nuova*, we have already spoken. It may be sufficient here to add that—though there is some controversy on the point—the name probably means only "Early" or "Fresh Life." The book was pretty certainly written not much after 1290, though the last chapter, in which the author's design to compose a greater work is alluded to, may have been added when the scheme of the *Commedia* was more developed. The *Vita Nuova* was not printed till 1578.

With regard to the date at which the most important of the prose works, known as the *Convito*, or "Banquet," was composed, considerable uncertainty exists. Villani says that the odes to which it is ostensibly a commentary were written in exile. Some critics hold that it belongs, at all events in great part, to the "pre-exilian" period of Dante's life; while others place it as late as 1310. The late Dr. Witte regarded it as the middle division of what he called "Dante's Trilogy"—the drama, that is, of the development of Dante's soul. In this view, the early love portrayed in the *Vita Nuova* marks an age of simple faith, undisturbed by any doubt. The *Convito* (so far as it was completed) records a period of philosophical speculation—not actually adverse to the truths of religion, but seeking to establish these rather on the basis of human reason than on revelation. Lastly, the *Commedia* shows us the soul, convinced that salvation and enlightenment are not to be found on this road, returning again to child-like submission. There is no doubt an attractive symmetry about this arrangement, but it is open to some objections, one of them being, as a French critic said, that part at least of the *Convito* must almost certainly have been written after the date in which Dante's conversion is represented as having taken place. Nor is it an answer to say that, the action of the *Commedia* being purely imaginary, we need pay no attention to dates. For one thing, Dante is extremely careful, and with more success than any one without his marvellous "visualising" power could hope for, to avoid anything like an anachronism in the *Commedia*. If he allows no event, which, in the history of the world, was still future in 1300, to be referred to as past, why should he have allowed this in regard to events in the history of his own spiritual development?

The truth is, that all these elaborate and symmetrical theories prove too much; and what is worse, they all spring from an ignorance, or a neglect, of the great facts of human nature. The *Commedia* is, of course, full of expressions of contrition for former error; of frank recognition that the writer has gone astray in the past, and hopes to keep straight in the future. But might not any man, any thoughtful man at all events, of thirty-five years old and upwards, take Dante's words with perfect sincerity, as the expression of his own deepest thoughts? Why assume that the faults of which Dante repented with tears in the presence of Beatrice, were limited to a too great reliance on human reason, or to a secret leaning to the philosophy of Averroes? Were they not moral as well as intellectual? Whether the year 1300 really marked an epoch at which anything of the nature of what is now called "conversion" took place in Dante's mind, we cannot say. It pretty certainly corresponded with a decided revulsion in his political views. It cannot have been without a pang that he found himself obliged formally to break with the Guelf party, of which he had hitherto been a faithful member, and to cast in his lot with men whom he, doubtless, like those with whom he had all his life associated, regarded as a set of turbulent, over-bearing swashbucklers, trying with the help of foreign men and money to reimpose a feudal tyranny on a prosperous and free commonwealth. For this is the aspect in which the Ghibelines must have presented themselves to a Florentine burgher of the year 1300. No doubt the doings of the Black party would have taught him that overbearing and tyrannical ways, turbulence and swagger were not the monopoly of one side, and that the freedom and peace of Florence must, in any case, soon be things of the past. All the foundations of the earth must have seemed to him to be out of course, and we can well imagine that his thought may have been driven inward, and he may thus have come to recognise how far the school which he had followed, and the path upon which he had walked—not in philosophy only, but in all matters of conduct—had led him from the ideals of his early manhood and from the way of God. Thus he would naturally refer the vision, which, of course, contains an allegorical account of all this change or "conversion," if we may call it so, to that year the events of which had given the first impulse to it.

It is not, however, necessary to suppose that with

Dante, any more than with most men of a similar age, a conviction that he had hitherto been on the wrong track involved an entire break with former habits, at all events of mind and thought. He may very well have gone on stringing together the curious medley of learning which he had not unfitly called a "Banquet."* As we have said already, it looks very like the contents of a commonplace book, in which materials for other works—notably for the *Commedia*—were collected. Many of the views enunciated in it may well be those held by Dante long before, and subsequently changed, though he might not have taken the trouble to expunge them, even when stating a maturer opinion in a later work.

A good many of the difficulties which arise in the consideration of the dates of Dante's works,

---

* This may be a good point at which to say that we need not suppose because Dante employed the Canzoni as pegs upon which to hang the philosophical, astronomical, and other lucubrations of the *Convito*, that when originally written they were anything but exercises in the amatory style of composition usual in that age, whether inspired or not by any serious passion. He would have found no more difficulty in attaching subsequently a mystical and moral interpretation to them than divines had found in doing the same for the Canticles.

probably arise from oblivion of the fact that "publication" in our modern sense did not exist in those days. An author would no doubt give his manuscript to friends to read, as he went along; and, if they liked it, they would probably take a copy of so much as they had. Thus portions of a book would get about long before the whole was finished; and in this way the views which Dante expresses in the *Convito* upon the cause of the markings in the moon, the order of the angelic hierarchies, the nature of the Milky Way, and similar matters, may well have been known to many as held by him, and he may have known that this was the case. Subsequently, having changed his mind—it may be, even before 1300—he would take the opportunity of a part of the *Commedia* having got into circulation, to recant; and even so the original view might stand in the *Convito*, and appear in that work when finally produced. When we further remember that Dante left the *Convito* little more than begun, and consequently, no doubt, unrevised, it will be clear that very little inference can be drawn as to its date, from the fact that certain opinions expressed in it are retracted in the *Commedia*.

It would be truer to say that it had no date. It was first printed in 1490.

The *De Monarchia* is a complete treatise, in fact, probably the only work besides the *Commedia* which we can feel sure that we have in a form which it would have retained however long Dante might have lived. Enough has been already said as to its scope; it may suffice to add that the Church has never looked upon it with favour, which was probably the reason of its not being printed till 1559, and then in Germany.

The unfinished treatise known as *De Vulgari Eloquentia* had the curious fortune to appear in an Italian translation (1529) some fifty years before it was printed in its original Latin. It is a mos interesting little work, showing considerable acuteness of perception in regard to peculiarities of locat vernacular, and a general "feeling" for linguistic matters.

How do we know that all these works are Dante's? it will be asked. Here we rest on unusually sure ground, for which once more we have to thank Villani.

In the Chapter to which we have already more

than once referred, containing the notice of Dante's death, that historian gives a list of his works. " In his youth," we read—

"he made the book called *The New Life of Love*; and afterwards, when he was in exile, he made some twenty moral and amatory odes, very excellent; and, among others, he wrote three notable letters, one to the Government of Florence, lamenting his own exile without any fault; the second he sent to the Emperor Henry; the third to the Italian cardinals, when the vacancy occurred after the death of Pope Clement. . . . And he made the *Comedy*, wherein, in polished rhyme, and with great and subtle questions of morals, nature, and astrology, philosophy and theology . . . he composed and treated in one hundred chapters, or chants, concerning the being and condition of Hell, Purgatory, and Paradise. . . . He also made the *Monarchy*, in which he treated of the duty of the Pope and of the Emperor. And he began a commentary on fourteen of the above-mentioned moral odes, in the vulgar tongue, which, through his death supervening, is only completed for three. . . . Also he made a little work which he calls *De Vulgari Eloquentia*, whereof he promises to make four books, but only two are extant, perhaps by reason of his speedy end; in which, in powerful and elegant style, and with fine arguments, he examines all the vernaculars of Italy."

The last two paragraphs, it should be said, do not occur in all manuscripts. But, assuming them to be genuine, it will be seen that we have here an almost contemporary notice, with one or two exceptions, of all the main works now contained in the editions of Dante. The chief exception is the curious little treatise on physical geography, called *De aqua et terra*, which purports to be a lecture delivered by Dante at Verona, in the last year of his life; but this is of very questionable genuineness. It was first printed, indeed, in 1508, but no manuscript of it is now known to exist.

Of the other works, Villani's notice may be regarded as clear proof that they are what they profess to be; and incidentally it may be said that his mention of them has probably been of great service. Literary morality was sufficiently lax in the fourteenth and fifteenth centuries, and people's ideas as to the use that might legitimately be made of famous names differed considerably from those now in force. As it is, a good many compositions have passed under Dante's name, from an early date, which scarcely pretend to be genuine works of his. We can imagine what a temptation it would have been for some enterprising man of letters to complete the *Convito* or the *De Vulgari Eloquentia*, or even to add a canto or two to the *Commedia*, if there had been no record in existence to let the world know where the genuine ended and the spurious began.* Even this security, however, is not quite sufficient to set us at our ease in the case of the letters. True, we have three letters purporting to be the three which Villani mentions, as well as several others passing under Dante's name; but it is, of course, possible that the very fact of his mentioning them may have sufficed to set ingenious scribes at work to produce them. Manuscripts of them are very few, and they occur in company with other works which are undoubted exercises of fancy.

On the other hand, more than one writer of the fifteenth century professes to have seen letters of Dante's, of which no trace can now be found. That referring to the battle of Campaldino, for which Leonardo Bruni vouches, has already been mentioned; and Flavius Blondus of Forlì, a

* In the case of the *Commedia*, it would seem that Dante himself took measures to guard against interpolations. As is well known, he never uses any one series of rhymes more than once in the same canto; and, from the structure of the *terza rima*, it is impossible to introduce any fresh matter when the canto is once completed without violating this rule. This fact alone serves to convict of forgery the unknown person who inserted eighteen lines after *Hell*, xxxiii. 90, in one of the Bodleian manuscripts; as to which, see Dr. Moore's *Textual Criticism*.

historian about contemporary with Leonardo, speaks of others as extant in his time. These, if they could now be recovered, would be of the greatest interest, since they related to the obscure period immediately following the exile of the White party. Meanwhile the genuineness of the more important letters which we possess is perhaps the most interesting question which remains to be settled in connection with Dante's works.

Besides the prose letters, two poetical epistles are still extant, and these, strange to say, the most sceptical critics have so far allowed to pass unquestioned. There is something a little pathetic about their history. Two or three years before Dante's death, a young scholar of Bologna, known from his devotion to the great Latin bard, as Joannes de Virgilio, addressed an extremely prosaic, but highly complimentary, epistle to the old poet, urging him to write something in the more dignified language of antiquity. Dante replied in an "Eclogue," wherein, under Virgilian pastoral imagery, he playfully banters his correspondent, and says that he had better finish first the work he has in hand, namely the *Commedia*.

One more communication on either side followed, and then Dante's death brought the verse-making to a close. In his own pieces one is struck rather by the melody of the rhythm and occasional dignity of the thought, than by the classical quality of the Latinity. But they are unquestionably remarkable specimens of Latin verse for an age previous to the revival of classical study, and, we should say, far more genial and more truly Virgilian in spirit than the most polished composition of the Humanists.

It is not intended here to enter into any analysis or estimate of Dante's prose works. The former task is one which readers should perform for themselves. Nor need they find it too much for their powers. With all his obscurity of allusion, and occasionally of phrase, Dante is not really a difficult author. From his teachers, the schoolmen, he had learnt to arrange his matter with due, perhaps more than due, regard to order and symmetry; and consequently the attentive reader is seldom at a loss to know what part of the subject is, at any given place, under consideration.

Of the obscurity which results from over-elaboration of the thought, or from an attempt at originality of expression, Dante is, in his maturer works, singularly free.* It must be remembered, too, that very often phrases which look to us like "conceits" are merely instances of the employment of scientific and technical terms now obsolete, but then familiar to every cultivated reader.

For æsthetic, or, as it has been unkindly called, "sign-post" criticism—that which, under the guise of directing the reader's taste, often seems intended to call attention mainly to the acuteness of the critic's own perception or his delicacy of phrase—the study of Dante would seem to be a very unpromising field. The sentimentalist and the elegant craftsman in words seem out of place in the company of this uncompromising seeker after realities, this relentless exposer of shams.

* It is, perhaps, worth noting that as the tendency to *concetti* increased in Italian literature, Dante was more and more neglected. Only three editions appeared from 1596 to 1716. Curiously enough, there are two treatises extant which just correspond with the beginning and end of this period of eclipse. One of them is called *A Brief and Ingenious Discourse against the Work of Dante.* It was written by Monsignor Alessandro Cariero, and published at Padua in 1582. The arguments are of the feeblest and most pedantic kind; but it marks a stage in taste. The recovery is indicated by a *Defence of Dante Alighieri,* a lecture given by Dr. Giuseppe Bianchini to the Florentine Academy in 1715, and published three years later.

It is much better that the student should begin by understanding his author. When he has mastered the meaning, it will be time enough to begin to admire, whether it be the thought or the words, or the expression of the one through the other. For this reason we should strongly counsel beginners to read Dante himself first, and books about Dante afterwards. We would go so far as to say: at the first reading, dispense even with notes, and be content to look out the words in a dictionary. It is far better practice to find out for yourself where the difficulties lie, than to be told where to expect them. Similarly with the "beauties." These will reveal themselves *a ciascun' alma presa e gentil cuore*, and every reader will find them in such measure as he deserves. Then will be the time to use the commentaries to solve, so far as may be, the problems which have been discovered, and then to take up such works as Mr. Symonds's *Study of Dante*, Miss Rossetti's *Shadow of Dante*, and Dean Church's *Essay*. The student who, to a thorough knowledge of the poem, joins a careful perusal of these three works will find his knowledge co-ordinated, his grasp of

Dante's whole system strengthened, his perception of Dante's greatness marvellously quickened. If he afterwards cares to pursue the subject further into the thickets of modern Italian and German criticism, he will find plenty of entertainment. Only let him remember that most of the minute details with which the excellent critics deal are not really of the very slightest importance.

As has been said above, there is ample reason for believing that the person to whom Dante refers under the name of Beatrice was a young lady of that name, daughter of one Folco Portinari, and wife to Simone de' Bardi. But suppose that irresistible evidence to the contrary could be found? Suppose that documents should come to light showing that no Beatrice Portinari ever lived—even that there was no woman, young or old, in Florence, who bore the Christian name of Beatrice between 1200 and 1300, what would it matter? Do we read Andromache's

"Hector, but thou to me art father and mother and brother, and thou my gallant husband too;"

or Helen's

"Hector, dearest to me by far of all my brothers-in-law, it

is now twenty years since I left my native land, but never yet have I heard from thee an ill or insulting word,"

with any the less emotion because we do not feel sure that Hector, or Andromache, or Helen ever lived on this earth? Some would add, or Homer; but so far, happily, no "separatist" has taken Dante in hand. But again, suppose he did, and with better success than has on the whole attended those who would have us believe that half a dozen or more men contributed to the *Iliad*, any one book of which would entitle its author to rank among the great poets of all time? The world would prove to be richer by as many great poets as could be shown to have collaborated in the writing of the *Commedia;* and how should we be the poorer? The poem would still be there, with all its power to soothe, to stimulate, to throw light upon the most hidden corners of the human soul, to reveal our own motives to us. It is, of course, only human nature to feel a personal interest in the man who has taught us so much; but we must not allow this natural sentiment to make us forget that the man is only interesting because of his work. After all, when the most destructive criticism has done its worst, we know much more about Dante than we know about the still greater Shakespeare; and let us be thankful for what knowledge we have.

APPENDIX I.

SOME HINTS TO BEGINNERS

SOMETHING has already been said as to the way in which the student of Dante should set to work in the way both of putting himself so far as possible at Dante's point of view with regard to earlier literature, and of availing himself of the various commentaries and treatises which subsequent writers have produced in such abundance; but it may be convenient to enter into this matter somewhat more in detail. It would obviously be too much to expect of every beginner that he should prepare himself for the study of Dante by a preliminary perusal of all the books which Dante may have read. But if he is to read with any profit, or indeed with any real enjoyment, some preliminary study is almost indispensable. Take, for instance, the historical standpoint. Some of Dante's grandest apostrophes fall flat to one who has not grasped the mediæval theory of the Roman Empire, as set forth in Mr. Bryce's well-known book or elsewhere. Much of his imagery, especially in the first Cantica, seems fantastic and arbitrary to one who is not familiar with Virgil's sixth *Æneid*, and does not realise that nearly every feature in the Dantesque Hell is developed, with assistance no doubt from mediæval legend, out of some hint of the Virgilian nether world. Of allusions to contemporaries it is hardly necessary to speak; and in many cases we must fall back on the commentators, who for their part have often nothing to tell us but what we have already gathered for ourselves. Cacciaguida's statement that no souls had been shown to Dante save those of people known to fame, may not be always true so far as any but the most strictly contemporary fame is concerned, but it is true in a great many cases. Few indeed there are whose names have not gained additional celebrity from Dante's mention of them; but, on the other hand, there are very few whose memory but for it would have perished altogether; and the thrill with which the reader comes across an old acquaintance, marked by the unfaltering hand for renown or infamy, as long as men shall read books on this earth, is far more satisfying than the process of looking a person up because he is some one in Dante. It is therefore at least worth while, if not essential, to know something of the minuter contemporary history, and those who can read the seventh, eighth, and ninth books of Villani's *Florentine History* —not yet, unfortunately, translated into English—will find their reward.

Those, again, who wish to place themselves as nearly as may be at the point from which Dante looked at ethical and metaphysical problems, will hardly be satisfied with an occasional quotation from Aristotle or Aquinas. If, as may well be the case, they cannot spare the time for systematic reading of those somewhat exacting authors, they should at least be at the trouble of acquiring such a knowledge of their systems, and of the place which they hold in the widening of men's thoughts, as may be obtained from Ueberweg or some other approved history of philosophy. So for physical science and natural history, those who have not the leisure to read Aristotle (again), or Pliny, or Brunetto's *Trésor*, may get from the fourth book of Whewell's *History of the Inductive Sciences*, and from parts of Humboldt's *Cosmos*, some idea of the way in which Dante would regard the external world.

But one book, among all others, was undoubtedly the main instrument in the formation of Dante's mind and character. Few professed Churchmen have ever been so saturated with the language and the spirit of the Bible as this lay theologian. It was this, indeed, which seems to have specially impressed his contemporaries. "Theologus Dantes nullius dogmatis expers" is the title which the epitaph of his friend Joannes de Virgilio confers upon him in its opening line. And among all the books of the "Sacred Library," as an earlier age called it, we can see that two had a predominant place in his memory—the prophecy of Jeremiah and the Book of Psalms. In these two we may find the solution of some of his most obscure symbolism, and careful study of these will do perhaps more than anything to help the student to read with understanding. Of course those who read Latin should use the Vulgate rather than the English version, for the key to an allusion sometimes lies in a word or a phrase, the identity of which is lost in an alien language.

It is with the study of such books as these, carried as far as the student's opportunities will allow, that he will best prepare himself for that of the *Commedia*. The next thing will be to read it, either in a translation, or better, in the original, working rapidly through the poem, and noting difficulties which occur, but leaving them for the present. He will thus get a comprehensive view of its general structure and scope, and probably find himself enthralled by the spell; after which, to put it on the lowest ground, he will have a subject of interest to investigate which will last him his lifetime. At any rate he will pretty certainly resolve to go over the ground again, this time more deliberately. Now will come the turn of the commentators, including under this term not only the actual annotators of the text, but those who have in any way discussed, explained, or interpreted the whole poem or its parts, either from a general literary point of view, or in the attempt to clear up special points. Of these there is no lack. Probably no great writer has given occasion for so much writing on the part of lesser men. The French critic Sainte-Beuve remarked that " to read Dante was almost inevitably to want to translate him; " it certainly seems as if to read Dante made the desire to write about him almost irresistible. Many of these books the world has pretty willingly let die; but a few will be read as long as Dante is studied in England. Foremost among these is the *Essay* by the late Dean of St. Paul's, Dr. Church. This is printed in a volume with an excellent translation of the *De Monarchia*. As an introduction to Dante from every point of view, whether in connection with the history of his time or in regard to his place in literature, it remains unrivalled, and is likely to remain so until a writer on Dante arises equal to Dean Church in acuteness of historical insight, delicacy of literary taste, and a power of expression capable of translating those gifts into words. No student should fail to read it; and those who can buy a copy will not be likely to regret the outlay. Another instructive book is the late Miss Rossetti's *Shadow of Dante*. It treats the poem rather in its religious than in its historical or philosophical aspect; and it is of especial value as an aid to understanding the often very perplexing symbolism. Long extracts are given from the versions by Mr. W. M. Rossetti (for the *Inferno*) and Mr. Longfellow (for the other parts); and these are linked together by a connecting summary. Mr. Symonds's *Introduction to the Study of Dante* is also useful, especially from the literary point of view, but it is occasionally inaccurate. Of actual translations none is better than Cary's, and this has most valuable notes.

These are some of the books from which a student, who did not feel equal to a preliminary study of Italian, might get information about Dante. It is to be hoped that there are not many who will stop here. When the genius of a poet is so closely involved as it is in Dante's case with the genius of the language, it cannot be too strongly impressed upon the student's mind that he ought to be read in his own words. Italian is the easiest to learn of all European languages, and the one in which the preliminary labour of learning grammatical rules is least required. Its grammar is very straightforward; its construction, in the best writers, is seldom involved; its words will in most cases be intelligible to people who know any Latin or French. The prepositions and their uses offer almost the only stumbling-block which cannot be surmounted by the aid of a pocket-dictionary; and even here the difficulty is more likely to be apparent in writing Italian. In reading, the context will usually be a guide to the meaning when the words are known.

The first thing will be to get a text. There are several modern texts published in Italy; but none of them are very correct. Giuliani's is an attractive little book; but the Abate was a somewhat reckless emendator, and some of his readings are very untrustworthy. The little pocket edition published by Barbèra contains Fraticelli's text, which suffers rather from lack of correction. Messrs. Longmans publish one based on Witte, but embodying the results of later inquiry. A complete text of Dante's entire works has lately been issued by the Clarendon Press, for the accuracy of which the name of its editor, Dr. Moore, is a sufficient guarantee. The "student's" editions with notes are those of Bianchi and Fraticelli, both in Italian. The latter is for some reason more popular in England, but the notes seem to me decidedly less helpful than those of Bianchi based on Costa's. Better than either is the *Vocabolario Dantesco* of Blanc. The original work was written in German, and no doubt is to be obtained in that language. It is really a very useful commentary, and has the additional advantage that it forms a pretty copious Concordance, and enables the student to compare the various uses of a word.

The student may now be supposed to be ready to set to work. How is he to proceed? This is a question very difficult to answer. Probably no two grown-up people will attack a new author, or a new language, in quite the same way. The present writer began Dante with very little knowledge of Italian; but knowing French and Latin pretty well. Being in Florence one day, he went to a bookstall and bought for one *lira* a secondhand copy of a little text published in 1811; and began to puzzle out bits here and there with the help of a small dictionary. In the following winter he went through the whole poem in Bianchi's edition with a friend, aided by various of the older commentaries. Then he took to reading the poem by a canto or two at a time, in bed, without notes or dictionary, and went through it two or three times in this way, at last beginning to feel that he would like to know something about it. Probably a course of this kind, spread in a rather desultory fashion over several years, would hardly suit every student. Nevertheless it has in its general features some merits. In the first place, the only way to learn is to find for yourself where the difficulties are; and this can be done most effectually by beginning with the minimum of help. With notes, there is always the temptation to look at the note first and the text afterwards: a process sure to result in slipshod and inaccurate knowledge. Take a canto at a time, and read it through. Go over the ground again with a commentary and perhaps a translation. Before long the difficulties arising merely from the language will be pretty well mastered, and progress will be more rapid. Above all, avoid in the first instance anything of the nature of æsthetic criticism. Be content to treat the poem, if it be not profane to say so, as a "grind." Translate into the plainest English, so only that you take pains to render every word. It is a very good exercise to keep to the same English word for the same Italian word. This will not be quite always possible; but on the whole it is wonderful how many words in Italian (or any other language) have passed through the same change of signification as some one of their English equivalents. (Thus "sorry" in English means both "sad" and "contemptible." You will find that Italian "*tristo*" bears both senses equally well.) Try to "explain Dante by Dante," that is, look out for peculiar phrases and constructions which may occur more than once, and get at their meaning by comparison of contexts. One great advantage possessed by the student of Dante is that his author is practically the first in the language in point of time; and though later Italian poets used Dante freely as a quarry, they did not do it intelligently. It may safely be said that, with the occasional exception of Petrarch, no subsequent Italian poet threw the least light on the interpretation of a single word in Dante. Indeed our own Chaucer seems to have understood and appreciated Dante far better than did Dante's countryman Ariosto. It is thus possible to read Dante without a very wide acquaintance with Italian literature in general.

Then, again, beginners need not be at too much pains to follow out the often very elaborate symbolism. On a first reading take the story as it stands. Let the dark wood and the three beasts, and the hill illuminated by the rising sun, remain what they profess to be, until you see the broad outlines of the poem. There are quite enough passages of purely human interest to occupy you at first. Francesca, Farinata, the Counts of Montefeltro, father and son, Ugolino, the assembled princes awaiting their time to enter Purgatory, the great panegyrics of St. Francis and St. Dominic, these and the like are the "purple patches" on which the beginner's attention should be fixed.

The student who has gone through the poem on these lines will by the end of it be ripe for a more thorough reading and a fuller commentary. Among modern commentaries the fullest is that of Dr. Scartazzini. He is a guide whose judgement is perhaps not always quite equal to his erudition; but his Commentary (in four volumes, including the *Prolegomeni*) is almost indispensable to the advanced student. He has also published an abridgement in one volume. Those who read German should make acquaintance with the translation and notes of the late King John of Saxony, who wrote under the name of Philalethes, as well as with those of Dr. Witte. Both these deal fully with historical matters, "Philalethes" also going very fully into the theology. In the present writer's edition some attempt is made to clear up obscure points of allegory, and to show the extent of Dante's debt to Greek philosophy. Attention is also called to questions of grammar and philology, which have been somewhat neglected by the Italian and German commentators.

APPENDIX II.

DANTE'S USE OF CLASSICAL LITERATURE

A FEW words on the mythological and classical allusions in the *Commedia* may be useful to those who are not familiar with Greek and Latin literature. The subject is a very wide one, and Dante's treatment of heathen mythology is very curious. It is especially noticeable in the *Purgatory*, where every sin and its contrary virtue are illustrated by a pair of examples from Scripture history on the one hand, and Greek or Roman history or legend (for both seem alike to him) on the other. Sloth, for instance, is exemplified by the Israelites who "thought scorn" of the promised land, and the slothful followers of Æneas, who hung back from the conquest of Italy; while Mary going into the hill country with haste, and Cæsar dashing into Spain are the chosen models of prompt response to the call of duty. So, again, at the very outset of the poem, we find St. Paul and Æneas quoted as the two instances of living men who have been permitted to see the future world; and Dante professes his own unworthiness to be put on a level with them, apparently without a hint that he holds the *Æneid* any lower as an authority than the Epistle to the Corinthians. In a practically pagan humanist of the days of Leo X.

this would hardly surprise us; but it is, at first sight, not a little astonishing in the case of a poet to whom the Christian Church and Christian revelation were vital truths. It is, however, clear that to the mediæval mind the Bible, though no doubt the highest authority, was in matters of morality, and to some extent even of theology, only "first among its peers." Aquinas quotes Aristotle, the Scriptures, and the Fathers almost indiscriminately in support of his positions. Dante, approaching the subject from a political as well as a moral point, takes for his guide and philosopher the poet Virgil, who, as the Middle Ages deemed, had both foretold the glories of the Church, and sung of the first origin of the Empire. It must never be forgotten that, to Dante, Church and Empire were merely two aspects of one Divine institution. Brutus and Cassius are hardly less guilty than Judas; and that simply from the official point of view, for there is no attempt to sanctify, much less to deify, Cæsar as an individual. None the less is the work that he did holy, and this holiness communicates itself, as readers of the *De Monarchia* will remember, to the whole of the long course of workings by which Divine Providence prepared the way for it. The finger of God is no less plainly to be seen in the victory of Æneas over Turnus or of the Romans over the Samnites than in the passage of the Israelites across the Red Sea, or the repulse of the Assyrians. Roman history is no less sacred than Hebrew. This being so, we shall not be surprised to find that a certain authority attaches to the literature of either one of the chosen peoples.

Did they conflict, doubtless the poet, as an orthodox Catholic, would admit that Virgil must give way to Isaiah; but he would in all probability decline to allow that they could conflict, at all events within the region common to them both. No doubt, just as Cæsar and Peter have, besides their common domain, functions peculiar to each, wherein Cæsar may not interfere with Peter, or as Aristotle may err when he trespasses on ground that the Church has made her province (for I interpret *Purg.* xxv. 63 as an allusion to Aristotle), so might Virgil or Lucan become a teacher of false doctrine if he ventured to teach theology. (Statius, who does teach theology, as in the passage just referred to, is, it must be remembered, a Christian.) But Virgil at all events holds scrupulously aloof from any over-stepping of his functions; and within his own limits his authority is infallible. Why, then, should we not accept his account of the infernal regions as trustworthy? He tells us that Charon is the ferryman who carries the souls across to the nether world; Minos the judge who sentences them; Pluto (whom we confuse perhaps a little with Plutus) a great personage in those regions. Furies sit over the inner gate; Gorgons and Harpies play their parts. Holy Scripture has nothing to say against these conceptions; so there is nothing to prevent our accepting Virgil's account, and expanding it into mediaeval precision and symmetry. Thus we have all the official hierarchy of hell ready provided. As has already been observed, it is not until Dante reaches a point very far down that anything like what we may call the Christian devil appears.* Throughout the upper circles the work, whether of tormenting or merely of guarding, is performed exclusively by beings taken from classic mythology. If we except the Giants, who seem to occupy a kind of intermediate position between prisoner and gaoler, Geryon is the last of these whom we meet; and him Dante has practically transformed into a being of his own invention: for there is little in common between the personage slain by Hercules and the strange monster with the face of a just man and the tail of a venomous scorpion. As might perhaps be expected when there was plenty of material to hand in Tuscany, less use is made of the persons of classical mythology in finding subjects for punishment. Among the virtuous heathen several find their place; but it may be doubted whether Electra or Orpheus were to Dante any less historical than Plato or Seneca. Semiramis, Dido, Achilles, again, would all be recorded in the histories of Orosius and others whom Dante read, with dates and possibly portraits. Capaneus, one of the "Seven against Thebes," is more nearly mythological; but as the utterer of the earliest profession of reasoned atheism † he could hardly be omitted as the typical blasphemer. The most curious example of all is the Thais whom we find among the flatterers. She does not attain even to the dignity of a myth, being only a character in a play of Terence, and borrowed by Dante from Cicero; probably the strangest instance on record of the "realization" of a dramatic personage.

* See p. 102.
† "Primus in orbe Deos fecit timor" (Statius, *Thebaid*, iii. 661).

www.ingramcontent.com/pod-product-compliance
Lightning Source LLC
Chambersburg PA
CBHW020900230426
43666CB00008B/1253